BETWEEN BLACK AND WHITE

HENRY HUGH PROCTOR

BETWEEN
BLACK and WHITE

AUTOBIOGRAPHICAL SKETCHES

By

HENRY HUGH PROCTOR

The Black Heritage Library Collection

BOOKS FOR LIBRARIES PRESS
FREEPORT, NEW YORK
1971

First Published 1925
Reprinted 1971

Reprinted from a copy in the
Fisk University Library Negro Collection

INTERNATIONAL STANDARD BOOK NUMBER:
0-8369-8903-1

LIBRARY OF CONGRESS CATALOG CARD NUMBER:
79-173611

PRINTED IN THE UNITED STATES OF AMERICA
BY
NEW WORLD BOOK MANUFACTURING CO., INC.
HALLANDALE, FLORIDA 33009

TO

MY FATHER AND MOTHER,
MY WIFE AND CHILDREN, MY PARISHIONERS
AND FRIENDS, AND TO
ALL OF WHOM MY LIFE HAS BEEN A PART

FOREWORD

Part of this narrative was published serially in *The Congregationalist.* The widespread and kindly reception given it there has emboldened me to give the rest of it here.

The career here described from the backwoods of the South to the Metropolis of the Nation may throw some light on the great migratory movement of the Negro people. Incidentally, some sidelights may be thrown on the greater world problem of color.

Certainly, the motive of it all has been to promote cooperation between Black and White whether in the South or the North, at home or abroad. And I see no better objective for the future. Hence, the title of this book — *Between Black and White.*

I want to thank Dr. Samuel Parkes Cadman for his generous words of introduction, which follow here. Since he penned these he has been made President of the Federal Council of Churches of Christ in America; but his permanent fame will rest on his services as Pastor of the Central Congregational Church of Brooklyn. Between his church and mine there is a beautiful spirit of cooperation. It is now an established custom to have a union service between the Central and Nazarene Congregational churches once a year. In this unique service there is full cooperation in pulpit, choir, and pew. The church is the mother of all good, and the movement of interracial cooperation should begin at the house of God.

HENRY HUGH PROCTOR

Borough of Brooklyn, City of New York
September, 1925

INTRODUCTION

Henry Hugh Proctor's life grasps the center of the Christian circle and touches its circumference at an amazing number of points. Born and bred in the narrowest and most unpromising surroundings, nevertheless this man has been enlarged on every side until he is now the leader of his people in the principal city of the United States of America. The secret of his career, and of its catholicity of service, is found in its religious starting place. Doctor Proctor began at the Cross where he determined to live sacrificially. His solicitude for the good of all men and, specifically, for the elevation of his own race, explains his noble words and deeds. The "desperate tides" of the world's woe and suffering have "crushed through the channels of his single heart." He has also visualized the goal ahead, where racial brotherhood shall dominate all separatism and prejudice. As his colaborer in the gospel, I gladly write this word of introduction.

S. Parkes Cadman

Central Church
Brooklyn, New York

CONTENTS

THE LIGHT OF THE BACKWOODS

CHAPTER I

The Light of the Backwoods

TEST almost any audience of colored people in the North, East, or West, and you will find the persons composing it have come from almost every state in the Union, particularly from the South. But you will discover from the uplifted hands that more come from Virginia in almost every case than from any other commonwealth. The reason is clear. The Old Dominion was the gateway to the New World for the African. It was in Virginia that the Dutch slaver landed the first group of African slaves a year and a half before the Pilgrims landed at Plymouth.

I trace my ancestral strain from Old Virginia. My father was born in South Carolina, and my mother in Mississippi, and they met in Alabama, where before the war my two brothers and two sisters were born. After this they moved to Tennessee, where, after the manumission of the sixties, I was the last born of my family. One day after I had seen something of the bigger world, my father showed me the ruins of the cabin in which I first saw the light. I see it now.

It stood back from the big road on a lane. Immediately around it were deep gullies cut by the torrents, but in the distance were the deep forests, and farther away the beautiful blue hills for which Tennessee is noted. Nearby ran Swan Creek, a stream of uncertain volume in the summer, but in the time of freshet overflowed all its banks, challenging the height of the overhanging cliffs.

But the first place where I remember anything was some miles away, where the family later moved. Our double cabin sat in the midst of a deep forest of beech trees, which seemed to me full of wonder. Occasionally a traveler would go by, and nothing delighted me more than to trace the steps of the horses in the sandy road. If a little colt followed its mother the curiosity of the pursuit was greatly increased. There in the forest I played alone, and was happy all the day long, until my brothers and sisters returned from the field. Saturday was a memorable day, when my sisters would do the baking for the Sabbath. How well I remember the cookies they made in the shape of animals, and hid away until Sunday! Sabbath was the day when company came, and I recall with vivid memories how I stood at the door of the cabin and wistfully watched the preachers tell stories and eat the last piece of fried chicken.

4

HENRY HUGH PROCTOR
As a boy in the backwoods of Tennessee

The Light of the Backwoods

The first deep impression of my life was made in these days. I recall it as if it were yesterday. I was in the field with my father, and I noted a dark patch of cloud in the sky about the size of a man's hand. It grew larger and darker until the whole face of the sky was covered. The thunder began to reverberate and the lightnings to flash; then came the rain. We sought shelter in an old unused house in the center of the field. The lightning became more vivid, and the thunder tones deeper. The artillery of the heavens seemed to be in full play. As I lay there beside my father in wonder nothing seemed to me could be more impressive. Somehow I was not afraid; perhaps it was because I was with my father; or it may be I learned that day to trust in a power higher than man. At any rate, that day I learned to love the storm, and have loved it ever since. Perhaps that is why I was not afraid years later in a storm on the Atlantic.

Later we moved some five miles away near a little place called Clifton. Our two-room cabin was in a beautiful valley. Behind our house was a low hill and in front of it rose another much higher, over which the sun stole every morning. It was from this place that I went to my first school. When my brothers and sisters went to the school five miles away I wanted to go too. My mother was reluctant to have me start because of my youth, but in view of my persistence she yielded. After the novelty of the first day I was not so keen to go the second, but my mother insisted that having started I should keep it up.

I recall that I lingered behind until the others left me. Just over the hill was a deep ditch which had to be crossed by a foot-log. There had been a rain the previous night, and the rails spanning the ditch were a bit slippery. The suggestion came into my mind to tell my mother that I had fallen from the rails into the ditch and thereby receive immunity from school attendance that day. Dressed in white I returned home without a speck of mud on me, and told my elder sister that I had fallen into the ditch. My mother came out and seeing my immaculate appearance realized what I was trying to put over on her. Taking in the situation she suited the action to the need, and began to apply a birch. I supplied the exclamation points, and when she finished, I was happy to start all over again. I ran all the way to school, and I haven't got weary yet. My mother made a man of me that day.

I wish I could describe that first schoolhouse I attended. It was a log cabin by the

The Light of the Backwoods

roadside on the outskirts of a little town called Boon's Hill. It was well ventilated; one could throw a cat between the logs, and never touch a hair. It was admirably suited for the study of astronomy; for one could look up through the roof and see the glory of God reflected in the heavens. The benches were made of rails, with standards for legs. They were innocent of backs, and desks were unknown. The method used was antiquated, and there was little attraction for the youthful mind. The passing of a rumbling wagon would attract the attention of the whole school. I recall how one boy turned his head sidewise and put it through the opening between the logs to see a wagon go by. The teacher spied him, and without warning began to apply a birch to the end in sight, and it was with considerable difficulty that the luckless lad extricated his head while the fireworks were proceeding in the rear.

It was in a school like this, continuing only three months in the summer, when the crops were laid by, that I began my education. Here I learned my alphabet in the old-fashioned way; here I learned to read and write. And near this spot out under a big tree I made my first speech at a closing exhibition. It was also here that I heard my first sermon; for the same building was used

for the church as well as the school. I shall
never forget the weird impression made upon
my mind by the lugubrious tone of the minister, as he described the coming judgment,
which I supposed was just at hand. I could
not understand how everyone seemed so
unconcerned after what the minister had
said. I took him literally and seriously, but
alas!

At about this time two of the greatest men
I had known came into my experience. It
was the custom of the people to have occasional meetings on the Sabbath under the
trees, when people came from near and far
in great numbers. Only a small part of the
people attended the preaching, however, the
greater part taking advantage of the occasion
for social purposes. Among those who came
were two brothers by the name of Kelsoe.
They were distinguished from the others by
being able to write letters, and the people
gathered about them in great numbers to get
them to write letters to their friends, and to
read letters received from them. As they
wrote and read these letters they seemed to
be the most wonderful men in all the world.
I wanted to be like them. As they rode
away in their linen dusters they appeared to
me to carry away with them the interest of
all the gathering. The vision of these men

The Light of the Backwoods

filled my imagination as I lived the life of a country boy in the backwoods.

But these were days of joy. Fortunately, they were filled with hard work. They meant going to the mill, minding the cow, hoeing the cotton, husking the corn, and cutting the grass. At the age of eight I could do as much plowing as a man; my father made a plow just for my size. But there was sport, too. There were hunting and fishing, skating and swimming. It was just the right kind of life for a growing boy. The corn-field was my gymnasium, the river my bath-tub, and the awe-inspiring sky of stars my moving picture. I had plain food, plenty of sleep, and an abundance of fresh air — things for which I have ever been grateful.

It is said that God made the country, man made the city, but that the devil made the little town. The justification of this bit of satire finds itself in the fact that just a dozen miles from where I was born, in the little town of Pulaski, the Ku Klux Klan began. Two types of stories stand out in my youth. The first was concerning ghosts, in which the plain country people in my day believed almost universally. I used to sit by the fireside and hear such blood-curdling ghost stories that I was afraid to go to the back of the room to go to bed. Along with these were stories concerning the Ku Klux. As the years grew I realized that ghosts were myths, but the Ku Klux remain a grim reality. Vanquished by legislative act in Tennessee because of their lawlessness and terrorism, they have risen again in these days of reaction after the World War. But the same spirit of true Americanism that overthrew them then will reassert itself and rid our democracy of this irresponsible group of self-appointed regulators.

At about this time I had an experience that changed my life. I was twelve years of age when my father for the first time took me to town twelve miles away. I had heard much about the city, and the night before that eventful journey I was restless with anticipation. The next morning I sat beside my father as we drove toward the city. Passing with difficulty over the crude country roads, we eventually came to the turnpike, and the houses began to look better and the country better kept. Evidently we were getting into a new type of place to me. Finally we reached the outskirts of the city, and the houses began to thicken. At last we reached the hill that gave us a full view of the little city, and such a thrill passed over me as I had never felt before. All at once the vision rose before me. Such a bewilderment of houses, steeples, cupolas; such a commotion of people, vehicles, smokestacks; such a labyrinth of streets! I sat in silence, as later I sat before the Grand Canyon. I have since seen nearly all the great cities of the earth, but not one of them has produced in me the thrill I felt when I first saw that little city of Fayetteville of two thousand inhabitants. In that hour there came into my life a great unsatisfaction.

THE THRILL OF THE CITY

CHAPTER II

The Thrill of the City

THE thrill I felt when I first saw the city never left me; it became a passion, and, I hope, melted into the compassion I have always felt for the crowd. Even to this day I can never see a crowd that I do not feel within me an urge to rise and talk to them about the deepest things of my life.

But this sense of thrill I never mentioned to anyone, not even my parents. And yet it is a remarkable thing that soon after that they moved to the town. I cannot tell you how glad I was when they decided to do this. The motive of the decision is that which moves so many of my people to go from the country to the city, and that is that their children may have better educational advantages. While in the country I had only three months' schooling in the year, and that was between crops. It was not hard to forget between times what one learned in the all too brief term. My mother said to my father that they had spent all their lives working for other people; now they should spend the rest of it working for their children. On this decision turned the wonderful advantages I have

15

had to get that education that was denied to my parents.

Having moved to the city, my educational advantages, while not ideal, were a vast improvement over those in the country. The school building was fairly good for the times, the term ran for nine months, and the teacher was pretty well equipped. I completed the common school course in the city public schools, and afterwards had the opportunity of becoming the principal of this school. In this capacity I had the opportunity of teaching the children of some of the boys and girls with whom I had gone to school.

But before I became principal of this city school I had an apprenticeship in teaching school in the country districts. My first teaching was as an assistant, and then I was called to teach a little school out on Pea Ridge for the sum of twenty-five dollars per month, which at that time seemed to me a large sum. That reminds me of the first money I ever earned. Another boy and myself were hired to pull the weeds from the grass in a yard in the fashionable part of the city. Our wages were fifteen cents apiece, and I recall with what zeal we knelt all over that yard pulling the weeds from the grass. The money I received for this work seemed to me the prettiest money I had ever seen.

RICHARD PROCTOR
Father of Henry Hugh Proctor

The Thrill of the City

This admiration for money led me to be the victim of my first practical joke. I had a little white dog which I loved very much. While down town one day some white men offered to buy the dog from me, and offered me five dollars for him. Although I loved the little dog the price seemed so big that I was willing to part with him. They took my little pet into the rear of the room, while they were supposed to be getting the purchase money. I finally became restless and suspicious, and to my surprise my little dog came rushing out past me with a tin can tied to his tail. Thoroughly excited, the dog ran all the way home before stopping. That was the first deception practiced upon me, and I can never recall any anguish of heart I have ever felt compared with the pain I felt that day over that first deception. It seemed so heartless and cruel. But, alas, that was just the beginning of a knowledge of the evil of the world. Then I knew there was some territory not included in Eden. As I carefully untied that knot from my dog's tail new thoughts of the world came to me.

But this was not the only shock I received in those days. I had learned the idea of thrift, and I wanted to have some money in the bank, so the first money I made in teaching I put in the bank. I recall how the banker praised me when I put in the second month's installment. But within a few days the little town was startled by the closing of the bank, and my hard-earned forty dollars was lost. I have never received one penny of that money. Then I began to realize that all that glitters is not gold, but that was not to be the last time that I lost money by investment. Yet this was a peculiarly trying experience, not only because it was the first but also because I was laying it away to go to college with.

I shall never forget my experiences in teaching school in the country. One of the customs was to board around from house to house. It was considered a slight not to visit every family in the district and spend the night with them. In most cases this was very pleasant, but in the nature of the case there were some places not so inviting. Very frequently I was disturbed in the night by the "scarlet ramblers"; they seemed all the more carnivorous in those rooms kept especially for company, and they seemed to enjoy strange flesh. But my most exciting experience was the night I thought I discovered a snake in my bed. It was not unusual to see snakes crawling between the logs of the cabin where you were to stay. And, sometimes, they got into one's bed and coiled up. Awakening

18

in the middle of the night, and stretching out, my foot touched something soft and all coiled up. Fearing to move lest the snake might be disturbed, I lay rigid and called the man of the house, saying: "Come quick; snake in my bed; snake in my bed." He came, bringing a light, and sure enough, at my feet there lay coiled up a big black — cat! Then I learned my first lesson in psychology, although I did not know it by that name.

Some time before this I had one of the most thrilling experiences of my life. It was the occasion of my first ride upon the train. The night before this experience I was so excited by anticipation that I could scarcely sleep. When I did fall asleep I overslept myself, and when I awoke it was broad daylight. Fearing the train had left me I dressed hastily and rushed to the station. On the way the train gave a shrill call, and I felt sure I was left. But I struck a dog-trot, and at length reached the station, only to be startled by another call of the whistle. But I got my ticket, boarded the train, took my seat, and in about two hours the dinky little train pulled out. How I remember that ride of forty miles to Winchester! I have ridden a good many miles on the train since then, but no ride gave me the thrill that ride did. How tall the trestles seemed, how ex-

pansive the valleys, how high the hills! I
was down there some time ago, but the hills
had melted, the valleys had shrunken, and
the trestles had squatted — since forty years
ago!

Within one hundred square yards occurred
three experiences that vitally affected my
life. The first was the vision of the city
already described. It took place on the road
at the top of the hill as it descends to the city,
affording a fine panoramic view of the little
city nestling amid the hills. Near this point
stood the church used as a schoolhouse. As
I was coming to school one morning my
teacher overtook me, and he put his hand
upon my head. I am sure he was not con-
scious of the impression he was making.
But that touch awakened in me sensations
that have not yet died away. My teacher
loved me. Although that occurred many
years ago, I could take one to within ten feet
of the exact spot where it occurred. It was
the place of the touch of life.

The other experience was my conversion in
the church that stood hard by. From my
earliest recollections my father and mother
were Christians, and no meal was partaken
of without the traditional blessing. There
was occasional family worship. My parents
were careful to have me attend church, and

three times on the Sabbath, morning, noon, and night, my mother took me to church. Although it proved irksome then this has turned out to be one of the greatest things in my life. No matter where I am now, whether at home or abroad, I must go to worship on the Sabbath, and that very custom has made the week fresh and new. Traveling abroad, I have found it a good thing to cease sight-seeing on the Sabbath, and to wait and worship. I have noted a weariness on the part of others who failed to do this.

This regularity and frequency of attendance at worship developed in me the spirit of the place, and I recall how I longed to be a Christian. In the darkness of the times I went forward to the anxious seat for a week, night after night successively, seeking an emotional satisfaction. At last it came, for the Father accommodates himself to the weak, and I realized an inner revolution that changed my life. I recall that afternoon vividly. With the inner newness everything without seemed changed. My very hands looked new, and there was a beauty on the hills and a tenderness in the skies I had never seen before. I found myself in love with everybody, with all nature, and with God. The sermon would not meet tests of the modern discourse, but I shall never forget how the

minister told of the bountiful nature of the
Father, as he discoursed on the parable of
the Master in which he told how earthly
fathers would not give their children a stone
if they asked for bread, nor a scorpion if they
asked for fish. The conclusion was inevit-
able: "How much more will your heavenly
Father give good gifts to them that ask him,
even the Holy Spirit!" I can never read
that part of the Sermon on the Mount without thinking of that central experience in my
life. It was with peculiar satisfaction years
later that I stood on the Horns of Hattin,
where the Master uttered those words.

THE CALL OF COLLEGE

CHAPTER III

The Call of College

CONVERSION is the wakening up of one all over. In my awakened condition, I found my supreme desire was to get an education. Before me loomed the walls of the college. It came about in this way. There came from Nashville some professors to hold teachers' institutes. One of these had gold-crowned front teeth; this was the first time I had ever seen a man with gold teeth in his mouth, and it made a deep impression on my youthful mind. It served to attract me to the man, and to study him closely. I found him to be the most cultured and high-minded man I had ever known. This deepened in me the desire to go to a college, such as the one from which this man came.

Accordingly I got together all the funds I could, and the next spring I found myself in the Central Tennessee College at Nashville. By dint of economy I was able to get through the term. While there I was told that Fisk University was a better school than Central Tennessee College. I wanted the best, so I planned to go to Fisk the next fall. I was saving money to this end from teaching in the summer, when the bank in which I had deposited the earnings of two months failed. Undaunted, I set out for Fisk with the twenty-five dollars I had saved from the last month's teaching.

I have often looked at the picture, "The Breaking of Home Ties," and recalled the morning when I bade my parents good-bye to go to college. While my father was getting my belongings together to go to the station, my mother followed me to the gate, and, putting her hands upon my shoulders, said: "Never do anything, my boy, you would be ashamed to have your mother know." I have heard some of the great preachers of the world, but none of them ever made the impression on me that those words of my mother made. Mothers are the world's greatest preachers, and the hand that rocks the cradle still rules the world.

I shall never forget the day I went to Fisk. Though I had little money, I received a most cordial reception. I was given a chance to work my way through. My familiarity with manual toil stood me in good stead. I never walk over the macadamized walks in front of Livingstone Hall without remembering that I had a hand in building that walkway. I spent seven years at Fisk, and I enjoyed each succeeding year more than its predecessor.

During that time I dug ditches, set type, taught, and preached, to help pay my way. But I could not have gotten through without the generosity of friends from the North. It was with peculiar pleasure that I gave an address recently in Vermont to an audience in which the church was represented that helped me through. I was glad to make this acknowledgment in this personal and direct way.

Just after the Civil War a wonderful thing took place in our land. Far-seeing men realized that if the newly emancipated people were to become real American citizens, the battle of bullets must be followed by the battle of books, the era of destruction by that of construction. Accordingly forts were turned into school sites, and officers jumped from their saddles to become schoolmasters. They were joined by some of the finest women the North ever had. These schoolmasters and schoolmistresses set up a system of schools throughout the South that has done more toward the solution of the problem of the races than any other one thing.

When Lincoln ascended the morning after his assassination, his mantle fell on those crusaders who, before the smoke of battle cleared away, came South, and in the spirit of the Samaritan set the millions of freedmen on the road toward reading, reasoning, and righteousness. Among them were Armstrong, who went to Hampton; DeForrest, who went to Talladega; Ware, who went to Atlanta; Cravath, who went to Nashville; and a host of women whose hearts God had touched, angels of light and mercy.

Among the many schools established throughout the South, I may be pardoned for thinking that Fisk is the best. Here was held persistently from the beginning the idea of a full college course for the training of the leaders of a people. As a result Fisk built up an institution with a spirit that took deeper hold on the talented tenth of the race than any other school. It drew promising young colored men and women from every part of the Union. One of the distinct advantages of the school was the social fellowship with the very best youth of the race. With great wisdom the teachers made the social life of the school one of its main features. Another thing that made Fisk attractive was the emphasis laid on music. Its fame went around the world in the original Fisk Jubilee Singers, and the Fisk interpretation of the Negro melodies is still unique. But the Mozart Society of Fisk has made a reputation for rendering the classics with great discrimination and fervor.

The Call of College

I was greatly impressed in my early days at Fisk with the dignity of the seniors. When I entered in 1884 the school was having its largest senior class, numbering fifteen. As I saw these men walk through the chapel, I thought that to be a senior was the greatest thing to which a youth could aspire. Unfortunately, when I later became a senior, the dignity did not seem so great. And yet I recall the aspiration it gave me to feel at that time that I would be a senior, too. Toward that end I began to strive with all my might, and during the days of sacrifice I felt I was still amid the roses.

Among the young people attracted to Fisk was a young man from Massachusetts by the name of DuBois. Coming out of New England there was something about him no other seemed to possess. He was soon to be known as the most brilliant student in the school. He was a lively, jovial chap, and a speaker of great magnetism. But his chief gift was in writing. I doubt if any professor in the school was his equal in English. During the summer he taught school in the country, and on his return he brought back a great stock of incidents. Once he fell sick, and his life was almost despaired of. When he graduated the brilliant career he has achieved as the finest scholar of the race was confidently forecast. Fisk people have watched his career at Harvard, Berlin, Atlanta, and now at New York as editor of the *Crisis*. He has carried the Fisk standard to the heights.

But there were equally fine young women at Fisk, for Fisk has ever stood for the equality of the sexes. Among these was Maggie Murray, who later became Mrs. Booker Washington. It was with great struggle that she made her way through Fisk. I recall that she taught school one summer in my county. I had introduced her to the people of the district, and after she arrived they decided to take the money for the school term and build a house, thus depriving the children of any school at all that season. But she gathered them all together, made an address to the men that was so effective that they decided to build the schoolhouse with their own hands and let the school go on. It was this spirit that has made Mrs. Washington the strong helpmeet in building up Tuskegee and a leader of the women of her race.*

Space forbids me to tell of the many bright young men and women I met at Fisk. The two I have mentioned are typical. But a great deal of their success was due to their teachers, who I believe were the best teachers

* Since these lines were written, Mrs. Washington has entered upon her much deserved rest. Her body rests in Tuskegee beside that of her husband.

in the world. They came to their task from
love. Many of them could have commanded
salaries far in excess of those they were receiving, together with the social fellowship of
their own people. But these noble workers
braved poverty and ostracism that they
might serve. Of them the South was not
worthy, and, in some cases, not even the
North!

Two women at Fisk stand out in my
memory. One of these was Miss Helen C.
Morgan, who came from Oberlin, and taught
Latin on the dirt floor in the old Fisk school
before it came to its more commodious quarters. She is the first woman in America to
have been a professor in a coeducational institution. She refused a higher salary at Vassar
to teach the same subject. She builded her
life into the walls of Fisk. With her was Miss
Anna Cahill, later Mrs. Henry S. Bennett.
She brought to Fisk a thoroughness, a culture,
and a refinement that was rare, indeed. She
traveled through the North seeking funds for
worthy students, and through her efforts
many young men and women were able to
stay in school and complete their education.

Both these women lived for many years in
Livingstone Hall, with the young men. I
recall how they climbed snowdrifts in winter
with us boys, going to Jubilee Hall for meals.

Between Black and White

During all the years of their residence with
these young colored men I never heard the
least complaint by these women concerning
any ungentlemanly conduct by a single student. And is it not a singular commentary
that although hundreds of these women have
lived in schools in the South, being domiciled
in the same building with young colored men,
not one has filed a complaint against them!

Three men at Fisk stand out in my thought
as molding factors in my life. One of these
was Prof. Adam K. Spence. He was of
Scotch descent, and bore striking resemblance
to Andrew Carnegie. The great Iron Master
seemed pleased when I told him of my admiration for his fellow-countryman. Professor
Spence was an enthusiast in missions, a pas-
sionate lover of Negro music, and our beloved
teacher in Greek and French. Above all, he
loved fair play. It was one of his sayings
that if the Negro was inferior to the white
man, give him a superior training, and if he
was superior give him an inferior training,
but if equal, give him the same. I recall
that a great oratorio was to be given in one
of the theatres in Nashville, and the students
wanted to go, but the authorities refused to
give them seats except in the gallery. Some
of our teachers deplored the situation, but encouraged us to go, assuring us that it would

32

not be so always. The students finally decided to go. When they arrived at the building and took their seats in the gallery, they
saw many of their teachers in the pit, looking
up sympathetically. But in the midst of the
students in the gallery sat Professor Spence.
We did not blame them, but it made us love
him in a way we could not love them. He
shared our estate. He made us think of
Jesus. It is no wonder he had such power
over the students.

Another man that greatly shaped my life
was Prof. Henry S. Bennett, who was the
university preacher. His great sermons redeemed for me the idea of the ministry, and
laid in my heart the foundations of the desire
to be a preacher of the gospel. It was from
him I received my first lessons in theology
and elocution. He used the blue pencil on
our speeches, and his great word in training
us to speak was to "fire up." He was the
dominating spiritual and moral force at Fisk,
and gave a tone to the institution such as one
could not find even at Harvard or Yale.
Professor Bennett organized the Congregational Church at Fisk, and was an influential
factor in the Congregationalism of the State
and the South.

But the one man who had more influence
over my life than any other was President

Erastus Milo Cravath. For nearly a quarter of a century he dominated the institution, and in a real sense Fisk may be spoken of as his lengthened shadow. I had the privilege of sitting at his table for four years, and as his assistant carver, I came into closer touch with him than most students. He was a remarkable man in physical appearance, looking in his latter days like one of the prophets of old. His favorite character was Moses, and he used to quote with great emphasis: "In the beginning God." Later, when I went to Yale, I found there no man his equal in poise, dignity, and magnanimity. He was a real Christian statesman, and the most polite man I ever knew. He greeted every student he met with a military salute or the lifting of the hat. I saw him meet a colored washerwoman coming out of Jubilee Hall one day, and he lifted his hat as politely as if she were the queen of England. When he came to Fisk his hair was black, but when he died it was as white as snow, and his blood had turned to water. He gave himself for Fisk.

The formative days of my life were those spent at Fisk. The very place seems sacred to me. Every corner of the campus seems crammed with God, and every bush aflame with divinity. It was here that I experienced my call to the Christian ministry.

MRS. HENRY HUGH PROCTOR
With her daughter Lillian

The Call of College

Professor Bennett laid the foundations of the desire in my heart, and one morning Moody and Sankey came. The great evangelist told of the shepherd seeking the lost sheep, and his companion in song sang "The Ninety and Nine." He followed this with his famous rendition of "When the Mists Have Rolled Away." Snow covered the hills of Nashville, and the tower of the capitol was shrouded in mists driven before the sunshine. When that service closed I had made my decision to be a minister of the gospel, and from that hour my choice has never wavered. I still feel as I did in that hour that I had rather be a minister of the gospel than anything else.

Toward the end of my days at Fisk events were crowding thick and fast, as the channels of my life were becoming more clear. I have referred to the social life at Fisk. It is on the campus of schools like Fisk that the foundations of the home life of a people are being laid. Fisk has the finest set of young colored women anywhere in all the world, and he must be fastidious indeed who cannot find among them one to suit his fancy. It is a veritable flower garden. I flatter myself that I plucked the fairest flower in the garden. It was here that I persuaded Miss Adeline Davis, a graduate of Fisk and later a teacher in the institution, to become the com-

35

panion of my life, and she has stood faithfully by in all these years and has been the noble mother of my children. She is an embodiment of Proverbs thirty-one. I drew the first prize at Fisk.

THE APPEAL OF NEW ENGLAND

CHAPTER IV

The Appeal of New England

WHEN I had finished at Fisk it was only natural that my teachers, who for the most part had come from Oberlin College, should want me to take my theology at that institution. I listened to all the arguments in favor of Oberlin and against Yale. I appreciate the fine history of Oberlin, the first institution in the world to admit colored people and women on equality with white men. I like its fine missionary spirit, and it has been a great thing to walk under the Oberlin arch in memory of those who died abroad for the cause. I like the teachers of theology at Oberlin; there are men there who cannot be duplicated in any other seminary in the land. But I also reasoned that, the most of my teachers having come from Oberlin, Fisk was a miniature Oberlin. I wanted a different atmosphere, not that this was not good, but I wanted something different.

I shall always be glad I chose Yale. In the first place it is in New England, the most benevolent community in the world, and the fountainhead of most that is good in our civic, educational, and religious life. And, with all respects to Harvard, Yale is its greatest institution. I found it thoroughly democratic, and although there were many students from the South, one's color counted nothing against one, and nothing in one's favor. A man is a man at Yale. Even today Yale does not ask about a man's nationality or color. She is interested only in the aristocracy of character and brain.

I was received by both teachers and students with genuine cordiality. I remember that at the opening reception at the Divinity School, Dr. Samuel Harris, the noted instructor in Biblical theology, asked me from whence I came, and when I told him I came from the South, he looked up at my more than six feet and said facetiously, "I am glad to see you here, and I assure you that you stand as high as any man in Yale." This same cordial spirit was manifested by all the students with whom I came in contact. We slept in the same buildings, ate at the same tables, and recited in the same seats. The socials of the institution were open to all the students in the University, and we colored students (there were twelve in all in the institution) attended the socials just as did other students.

When we first entered the Seminary, however, there were some white students from

the South, and our presence seemed strange
to them. A certain student from Maryland,
now a metropolitan clergyman, came to our
room one day with a confession. He said
that he had never before seen colored people
in the capacity in which he saw us, that he
had only come in touch with them in the
kitchen and the stable, and that he thought
his mother was right in believing the Bible
justified slavery. Since he had been there,
however, and had seen colored students bearing themselves just like the rest, he had been
converted, and he was going back home to
convert his mother. After that he came to
our room, and we studied Hebrew roots together. We ate at the same table in the
restaurant. When a fire broke out in East
Divinity Hall, and we had to double up in
the West Divinity, I found myself a temporary roommate of this Southerner, and we got
along finely. When our class photo was taken
he came and sat near me. Later, when my
wife and I were in the city of Washington, he
came with his conveyance to show us the
courtesies of the city.

There were four of us colored students in
the Divinity School each year I was there,
and we formed a quartet to sing Negro melodies. We were soon invited to sing in the
local churches, and on one occasion we fur-

nished the music at the Divinity commencement exercises. Our reputation began to spread, and soon we had all we could do for three years. We used to go out on Friday afternoon and return Monday morning. In this way we visited nearly all the centers in New England. We received a most cordial welcome in the churches, and in this way the foundations of some of my most valuable friendships were laid. This also helped us pay our way through Yale. I sometimes say I dug my way through Fisk and sang it through Yale.

One of the four men that formed our quartet was Orishatukeh Faduma, a native of Sierra Leone, West Africa. Although his parents were natives taken right from the bush, he was one of the brightest men in the class of over thirty coming from the picked universities of the world. He upset all the theories of the phrenologists and ethnologists. He took a scholarship in Hebrew, and after a few years' work in the South returned to his native land, where he is the superintendent of education.

Before going to Yale I had heard much of the Yale theology, but when I got there I could find no particular brand. A new type of teaching had come in vogue. The professor did not try to put over any particular theory. It was the endeavor to make the men think out things for themselves and to come to their own conclusions. In the classroom there was the freest opportunity for discussion. On graduation day we were told by one of the professors in the graduating address: "Young men, we have taught you nothing; we have showed you where the ore is. Go, dig for yourselves." I have learned by experience that it is only that which I dig for myself that I treasure supremely and can impart with force to others.

The men at Yale in my day were giants. There was Professor Harris, who had written a number of books on the self-revelation of God, but it was agreed that his face was an even greater revelation of God than his books. There was Prof. George B. Stevens, an authority on the New Testament, and a man of great humanity. Prof. E. L. Curtis drilled us in the roots of Hebrew, and gave us an insight into the genius of the Hebrew mind. Prof. Frank Porter spoke authoritatively on the Old Testament. President Dwight lectured on John, and Dr. Day was the dean at that time. Prof. George Fisher lectured from his own books in church history. In our last two years Professor Curry, of the School of Expression in Boston, taught us how to speak. Among the chief lecturers in my day was

Between Black and White

Dr. Horton of England, whose coming was like a breath of fresh air from the other world.

One of the great opportunities at Yale was Battell Chapel. Here the great lecturers of the nation came and gave the best they had. The ablest ministers of the country came in turn to preach. Among the opportunities of New Haven were the churches of the city. The three main churches were on the Green, two Congregational and one Episcopal. But in addition to the churches presided over by Munger and Smythe, there were other churches such as those which Phillips, Twitchel, Luckey, and Mutch led. I frequently attended the church of which Rev. W. J. Mutch was pastor, and I was surprised to have him call upon me one day and ask me to fill his pulpit in his absence. This sense of impartiality made a profound impression upon me, as I was about the only student from the seminary who regularly attended this church. I was greatly impressed with the cordiality with which I was received at the Humphrey Street Church, of which Mr. Luckey was the eloquent pastor. Of course, I was found frequently in the colored churches, especially at evening time. The best colored church in that city was the Dixwell Avenue Congregational Church, of which Rev. A. P.

44

Miller, a fellow alumnus at Fisk, was the able pastor.

One of the advantages at Yale was its nearness to New York City, where we often went for special occasions. One of the most interesting occasions I attended in the metropolis was an evening in Cooper Union. The main speaker was Frederick Douglass. I had never seen the great leader of my race before. It was, therefore, with great interest that I looked forward to the evening when for the first time I should hear him. There were two other speakers that evening. One was Chauncey M. Depew, polished, graceful, forceful. The other was Robert Ingersoll, that great humanitarian, who had a higher ideal along race lines than many professing Christians I know. But Douglass was without question the greatest orator of the evening. As in his earlier days when an anti-slavery speaker, "he laid all the others in the shade."

My graduating thesis at Yale was on the theology of the songs of the slaves of the South. In this I tried to show how these slaves built their songs on a real theological system. In these songs I found thought, art, and heart conjoined. They formed the true American music, and they were singularly free from malice and ill-will. This was subsequently published in the Hampton *Workman*, of Hampton, Virginia. My study for this thesis gave me a new insight into the heart and life of my people.

It was the custom in my day at Yale for the faculty to choose eight speakers to represent the class on graduation day. I was surprised to find myself one of the number, and after rehearsal of our selections before the faculty I was given the post of honor of all the speakers. The subject of my address was "A New Ethnic Contribution to Christianity." In this address I tried to show that the Jew had given us ethics, the Greek philosophy, the Roman law, the Teuton liberty, and the Saxon enterprise, but that, in view of his nature, the Negro might be expected to bring to Christianity the new and needed contribution of love. This was later published in *The Congregationalist*. It is reprinted in the next chapter of this text.

A NEW ETHNIC CONTRIBUTION
TO CHRISTIANITY

CHAPTER V

A New Ethnic Contribution to Christianity

IN the historic development of Christianity
race and religion have had a reciprocal re-
lation. Conversion has involved a mutual
conquest. The religion has modified the race;
the race has, by developing that element of
Christian truth for which it has special affin-
ity, modified the religion. Every race that
has embraced Christianity has brought to the
system its own peculiar contribution.

In the Semitic race, the high priest of humanity, Christianity was born. "Salvation
is of the Jews." Israel's code of ethics was
the highest known to antiquity. It was but
natural that the Hebrew should leave upon
the new-born system the impress of his genius
for ethics.

Hellenism may be regarded as the comple-
ment and contrast of Hebraism. Hebraism
revealed the transcendence of Jehovah. Hellenism declared the divinity of man. The
Greek, preeminent in philosophy as a pagan,
became, as a Christian, preeminent in theology. He blended the conceptions of divinity and humanity. If the contribution of the

Hebrew was ethical, that of the Greek was theological.

The Latin mind, practical rather than speculative, political rather than theological, established the *Civitas Dei* where once stood the *Civitas Roma*. This ecclesiastical masterpiece of human wisdom "may still exist in undiminished vigor," says Macaulay, "when some traveler from New Zealand shall, in the midst of a vast solitude, take his stand on a broken arch of London Bridge to sketch the ruins of St. Paul's." Truly the Church of Rome has left upon Christianity an ineffaceable political impress.

The Teutonic mind — fresh, vigorous, even childlike in its simplicity and love of reality, accustomed to enjoy the freedom peculiar to lands where the national will is the highest law — would not brook the inflexible dogmatism of the Greek nor the iron ecclesiasticism of the Roman. The Teuton loved liberty in religion as well as in other things, and asserted his right to stand before his God for himself. The free spirit revealed in Christianity through Luther can never die. "Christianity as an authoritative letter is Roman; as a free spirit it is Teutonic."

The Saxon, preeminent in capacity for developing ideas, has so assimilated Christianity as to become its noblest representative.

A New Ethnic Contribution to Christianity

Enterprise and energy, vigor and thrift, striking characteristics of this great race, are becoming part and parcel of our Christianity. This is the missionary age, and it is the enterprising Saxon unchecked and undaunted by sword, flame or flood that is encircling the globe with a girdle of divine light.

And yet our Christianity is not complete. Notwithstanding its moral stamina, its philosophic basis and its organic solidarity, its free spirit and its robust energy, do we not feel that there is something lacking still? Does not our Christianity lack in its gentler virtues? To what nation shall we look for the *desideratum?* Shall it not be to the vast unknown continent? If the Jew has modified our religion by his ethics, the Greek by his philosophy, the Roman by his polity, the Teuton by his love of liberty and the Saxon by his enterprise, shall not the African, by his characteristic qualities of heart, bring a new and peculiar contribution to Christianity?

The Negro is nothing if not religious. He has a genius for religion. His religion touches his heart and moves him to action. The result of his peculiarly partial contact with Christianity is an earnest of what his full contribution may be expected to be. The African's mission in the past has been that of toil. "Servant of all" is his title. He has

51

Between Black and White

hewn the wood and drawn the water of others
with a fidelity that is wonderful and a patience that is marvelous. As an example of
patient fidelity to humble duty he stands
without a peer.

His conduct in the Civil War, which resulted in his freedom, was a bit of rare magnanimity. The helpless ones of his oppressor
in his power, he nobly stayed his hand from
vengeance. And at last, when he held up his
hands that his bonds might be removed, his
emancipator found them scarred with toil un-
requited but free from the blood of man save
that shed in honorable battle.

His religious songs are indicative of his real
character. These songs embodied and expressed the sentiment of the only public utterance of a people who had suffered two and
a half centuries of unatoned insult, yet in
them there has not been found a trace of ill
will. History presents no parallel to this.
David, oppressed by his foes, called down fire,
smoke and burning wind to consume his enemies from the face of the earth. But no such
malediction as that ever fell from the lips of
the typical American slave. Oppressed, like
the Man of Sorrows, he opened not his mouth.

Truth is stranger than fiction. Harriet
Beecher Stowe's "Uncle Tom" was more than
a character of fiction. He was a real repre-

52

A New Ethnic Contribution to Christianity

sentative of the Christian slave. Recall that scene between Cassy and Uncle Tom. Unsuccessful in her attempts to urge him to kill their inhuman master, Cassy determines to do it herself. With flashing eyes, her blood boiling with indignation long suppressed, the much abused Creole woman exclaims: "His time is come. I'll have his heart's blood!" "No, no, no," says Uncle Tom. "No, ye poor lost soul, that ye must not do! Our Lord never shed no blood but his own, and that he poured out for us when we was enemies. Lord help us to follow his steps and love our enemies."

Humility, fidelity, patience, large-heartedness, love — this is Africa's contribution to Christianity. If the contribution of the Saxon is Pauline, that of the African is to be Johannine. The Saxon and the African are contrasts, not contraries, complementary opposites, not irreconcilable opponents.

The Jew has given us ethics, the Greek philosophy, the Roman law, the Teuton liberty. These the Saxon combines in one. But the African — "latest called of nations, called to the crown of thorns, the scourge, the bloody sweat, the cross of agony" — the African, I say, has the deep, gushing wealth of love which is yet to move the great heart of humanity.

53

THE THEOLOGY OF THE SONGS OF
THE SOUTHERN SLAVE

CHAPTER VI

The Theology of the Songs of the Southern Slave

WHEN the Southern slave came forth from the house of bondage it was with a song in his mouth. It was the triumphant note of that ancestral strain which, caught up from sire to son and from matron to maid, found its long expected fulfilment in freedom's glad hour. For more than two centuries the slave had been singing and sighing. That he sighed was natural, but that he sang has not ceased to be the wonder of all thoughtful men. Every race, we are told, has passed through slavery; but for the Negro people was reserved the unique distinction of giving the world a body of song during the days of its bitter oppression. The American Indian oppressed sank in hopeless apathy, and during the days of oppression gave forth no note of song. The Jew, captive by the river of Babylon, when asked for a song, hung his harp upon the willows and refused to sing the song of Zion in a strange land. But the Negro, snatched from the bosom of his native land, transported to distant shores, subjected to a hard bondage,

Between Black and White

so sang that the world could not choose but hear. Thus wrote Longfellow, as he listened to a Negro singing across the rice swamp:

> "Loud he sang the Psalm of David,
> He, a Negro and enslaved,
> Sang of Israel's victory,
> Sang of Zion, bright and free.
>
> "In that hour when night is calmest,
> Sang he of the Hebrew Psalmist,
> In a voice so sweet and clear
> That I could not choose but hear."

From the standpoint of art the music of these songs has been a surprise. Says a musical critic: "From so unpromising a source we could expect only a mass of crudities unendurable to the trained ear. On the contrary, however, the trained listener confesses to a new charm and to a power never before felt." It is a noteworthy coincidence that most of these melodies are in the same scale as the primitive music of Scotland and Greece. Though the composers of these songs knew nothing of music as a science, yet when the scientific musician applied his standard he found but few cases of what theorists call mis-form, although "the student of musical composition is likely to fall into that error long after he has mastered the leading principles of the art." "The rhythm, though

58

often complicated and strikingly original,"
says one, "produces effects extremely satis-
factory." President Dvorak of the School of
American Music asserted that in these melodies lay the basis of a music distinctively
American. His first symphony developed
on the basis of these melodies received the
plaudits of the public and the unstinted
praise of musical critics.

But there is more heart than art in these
songs. The noble Christian sentiment in
them has filled more hearts than Longfellow's
with "strange emotion." A little child listen-
ing to the Jubilee Singers burst into tears.
When they sang before the Queen of England
she broke down and wept, saying, "Don't
think I am weak because I weep; your songs
have touched my heart." These songs came
from the heart, and they go to the heart.
They have the very tone of the gospel in
them. They breathe the odor of spiritual
sacrifice. As the bruised flower yields the
sweet perfume, and the crushed grape the
blood-red wine, so the hearts of these people,
bruised by oppression and crushed by ad-
versity's iron heel, poured forth the sweetness
and purity of the gospel in song.

Art, heart, and thought are joined in these
songs. They are to be admired for their art,
loved for their heart, and treasured for their

thought. They contain more religious and
theological truth than would at first be supposed. Not allowed to formulate his thought
in public address, the slave expressed his
sentiments in song. These songs were born
of necessity; human nature must have an
expression. The Negro was ever singing; he
sang of his troubles and hopes, his bondage
and his freedom. Mingled with these were
echoes of his struggles with sin, his striving
after godliness, his fleeing from Satan, his
search for God. So the student, tracing out
the intricacies of thought in these songs, may
find a system of belief. That this system was
more or less clear in the mind of the slave by
no means invalidates the claim of its existence. It is well known that one may speak
logically, and yet have no knowledge of logic
as a science.

The Bible itself is not a theological treatise.
The writers of that sacred Book would not be
considered theologians in the commonly ac-
cepted sense. The Bible is a collection of
deliverances, addresses, sermons, discourses,
songs, letters, and narratives. From these
the student constructs a theology of the
Books of the Bible — Biblical Theology.
Not dissimilar in kind, however unlike in
importance, is the task assumed in my attempt
to formulate a system of theologico-religious

conceptions from the songs of the Southern slaves.

THEIR BELIEF AS TO GOD

They believed that God revealed himself in nature. They believed with Pope that

> "He warms in the sun, refreshes in the breeze,
> Glows in the stars and blossoms in the trees;"

for in that remarkable melody, "Steal Away to Jesus," they sang:

> "Green trees are bending;
> Tombstones are bursting,
> Poor sinners stand trembling;
> My Lord calls me;
> He calls me by the lightning,
> He calls me by the thunder."

They also believed in a revelation of God in the consciousness of men. In the refrain of the same song they sang:

> "The trumpet sounds within-a my soul."

Indeed, they believed in a direct and immediate revelation, as is shown by a verse from another melody:

> "I wonder where Sister Mary's gone —
> I heard from heaven to-day;
> It's good news an' I thank God."

They believed strongly that God had all

power and perfect knowledge.   Listen as they
sing of his almighty power:

> "He is King of Kings;
> He is Lord of Lords;
> No man works like him,"

and of his perfect knowledge:

> "Oh, he sees all you do,
> He hears all you say."

From this would follow their belief that he
was everywhere present.   They saw God in
everything; he was everywhere.

Nor did they think of him merely as a great
and royal personage.   He was Father, and in
their trials he would be with them.   Observe
the faith and dependence they discover as
they cry out from the valley of their weeping:

> "Oh Lord, oh my Lord;
> Oh, my good Lord,
> Keep me from sinkin' down."

In their distress they cried unto the Lord,
and he heard them.   He who heard the
raven's cry could not be dumb to the cry of
the slave.   He kept them from sinking down,
and in his own time and way brought them
out of the Egypt of American bondage.

Theology of the Southern Slave Songs

They believed Jesus to be God's Son come into the world to express his Father's love and to bring back the sinning world to himself. That Christ had a double nature, though in what way was incomprehensible to them (as to us), was obviously their belief. They showed their belief in his divinity by ascription to him of supernatural power. He "rides in the middle of the air," "walks upon the water," "gives sight to the blind," "rids death of its terror." His resurrection and ascension furnished further proof of his divinity:

"The Jews killed poor Jesus, an' laid him in a tomb;
He 'rose, he 'rose, an' went to heaven in a cloud."

Again, they showed their belief in his divinity by the kingly qualities they ascribe to him. Listen as they salute their King:

"Reign, oh reign, oh reign, my Saviour,
Reign, Massa Jesus, reign!"

The atoning significance of his death gave proof of his divinity:

"Oh, redeemed, redeemed;
I'm washed in the blood of the Lamb."

Thus they bore testimony to his divinity by

63

their belief in his supernatural power, resurrection, royalty, regnancy, and atoning work.

But to them he was also human. He was
"a man of sorrows." He could sympathize
with those "acquainted with grief." How
solemnly and sweetly they sang of his cru-
cifixion:

"Were you there when they crucified my Lord?
 Were you there when they nailed him to the tree?
 Oh, sometimes it causes me to tremble, tremble,
    tremble."

In this suffering Saviour they found a friend:

"Run to Jesus, shun the danger,
   He will be our truest friend,
   An' will help us to the end,
      Run to Jesus."

The late Frederick Douglass was accustomed
to say that it was this hymn that inspired
him to run away from slavery in search of his
freedom. On this Friend they relied with
firmness and fullness of faith. If Jesus were
their leader they would walk "through the
valley of death in peace." With unwavering
faith they sang:

"Oh, when I come to die — give me Jesus, give me
   Jesus.
 You may have all this world, give me Jesus."

Jesus was their companion in the fields,

their help in trouble, their mediator before the Father, their hope of glory. To them he was the one sent to bind up the broken-hearted, to proclaim liberty to the captives, the opening of the prison to them that are bound; to comfort all that mourn; to give unto them the garland for ashes, the garment of praise for the spirit of heaviness, even as Isaiah wrote.

THEIR BELIEF AS TO THE HOLY SPIRIT

The slaves believed in the Spirit — the third person in the Trinity. Their songs, not unlike the Bible in this regard, nowhere contain the word trinity, nor have we any evidence that they knew that theologians had formulated such a doctrine; but if we examine their songs, we shall find material for the doctrine. They believed in the Father, the Son, and the Holy Ghost. The mysterious connection between these they did not try to find out. They were not troubled with Sabellian, Unitarian, or Trinitarian theories. But they believed in the Spirit as emanating from the Godhead. No one could be a Christian without the "witness of the Spirit in his breast." The divine Spirit must bear witness with the human spirit as an evidence of adoption. No one could preach without a direct revelation of the Spirit. No meeting was successful without an outpouring of the Spirit, which would make itself felt by physical excitement. Indeed, in their worship they approached the borderland of mysticism. As the exuberance of plant life bears testimony to the reality of rooting and the richness of soil, so their worship, exuberant and excessive though it often was, bore testimony to its genuineness and reality. It had its root in the supernatural. Excesses there were in their worship, and such need not be encouraged under the changed conditions of today; but was it not a kind providence of God that these unfortunate people could so lose themselves in their worship that they could forget the wickedness of this world, and for the time being at least become one with the Eternal? It kept them from sinking down.

But let their songs tell of their belief in the Holy Ghost:

> "When Peter was preachin' at Pentecost,
> He was filled with the Holy Ghost."

The following indicates their belief as to the nature, source, and conditions of reception of the Holy Ghost — "the heavenly breeze":

> "If you want to catch that heavenly breeze,
> Go down in the valley on your knees;
> Go bow your knees upon the ground,
> An' ask the Lord to turn you 'round."

Theology of the Southern Slave Songs

Hear them in their camp-meetings, when at the climax of a fervid gospel song their leader exclaims:

:"Oh! I feel the Spirit a-movin',"

and the choir, which comprises the whole audience, responds in the refrain:

"Don't you get weary,
There's a great camp-meetin' in the promised land."

To sum up: they believed in the Holy Ghost; they believed that he came from heaven, that he was received in answer to prayer in conversion, and that he operated in the human heart.

THEIR BELIEF AS TO ANGELS

Perhaps the most beautiful of all their doctrines was that of the angels. Angels were God's messengers. They stood for all that was beautiful and lovely. It was the angels that officiated at conversion:

"I went to the hillside, I went to pray;
I knew the angels done changed my name,
Done changed my name for the comin' day;
I knew the angels done changed my name."

Again:

"Those angels' wings are tipped with gold,
That brought glad tidin's to my soul."

Between Black and White

It was the angels that rejoiced around the throne when a sinner returned:

"Listen to the angels shoutin'!"

It was the angels that welcomed their departed ones to glory. At the death of a saintly sister they sang:

"My sister's took her flight an' gone home,
An' the angel's waitin' at the door."

It was the angels that would come and convey the righteous to the better land. This is set forth in "Swing Low, Sweet Chariot," that hymn which Mr. Gladstone always called for when the singers sang before him:

"I looked over Jordan, an' what did I see,
Comin' for to carry me home?
A band of angels comin' after me,
Comin' for to carry me home."

It was an angel, Gabriel, who would stand with "one foot on the dry land and the other on the sea and declare that time shall be no more":

"The Lord spoke to Gabriel:
'Go look behind the altar,
Take down the silver trumpet,
Blow your trumpet, Gabriel.'"

It was the angels who, when the world was on fire, the moon bleeding, the stars falling, and the elements melting, would attend the Saviour in the middle of the air to accompany the righteous home:

"Then you'll see my Jesus comin'
With all his holy angels,
To take the righteous home to heaven."

THEIR BELIEF AS TO THE CHRISTIAN LIFE

To the slaves the Christian life was the ideal one — a life of dependence, of trust, of service and communion; a life linked with God, the Infinite One. Communion through prayer was uppermost in their minds; a devout slave after being severely flogged would go behind his cabin and, sitting upon a certain log, would sing out his grief in a song of which this is a couplet:

"In the dark days of bondage to Jesus I prayed
To help me to bear it, an' he gave me his aid."

Or, again, in the song "Keep a-Inchin' Along":

"Trials and troubles are on the way,
But we must watch an' always pray."

It was a life of strict morality as well as of highly wrought emotion. It is often asserted by those partly informed or biased by prejudice that the Christian life as conceived by the slaves had no union with morality. That many of their practices were not in accord

69

with the decalogue no one will deny. What
society lays claim to perfection in this regard?
But to vindicate the practice of the body of
slaves is not the point at issue. To vindicate
the practice of any community would not be
a very easy task. The practice of the slaves
was greatly affected by their environment,
which few would claim to be ideal. The
question is, Did religion as conceived by the
slaves have an ethical import? It most surely
did, as will be illustrated presently by their
songs. Not only did their conception set a
high ideal upon godly living, but not a few
of them attained to a high standard of godliness. "Uncle Tom" was a real character.
There were slaves who prized personal honor
and integrity higher than personal freedom.
Unnumbered were the slave heroes who would
suffer before they would tell a lie. Unwritten
are the many instances in which slave women
bared their persons to the lash rather than
submit to the lust of the master for exemption
from drudgery, for ease, for luxury, for gold.
Unrecorded — save in the annals of God —
are the persecutions, the sacrifices and dangers
which the devout slave endured for the sake
of his religion. No wonder that an impartial
writer exclaimed: "Were I to search America
for its saints, I should not be surprised to find
some of them among the slaves of the South."

Theology of the Southern Slave Songs

But lest I wander afield let us examine their songs on this point; they speak for themselves. They pointed to the sayings of Christ as the Christian's guide:

"Go read the fifth of Matthew, and read the chapter
    through;
  It is a guide for Christians, an' it tells them what to
    do."

How is this for pointed moral exhortation?

"You say you're aimin' for the skies;
Why don't you stop your tellin' lies?

.   .   .   .   .

You say the Lord has set you free;
Why don't you let your neighbor be?"

These instances are not exceptional; their songs abound with them.

The Christian life was to them one of activity; their piety was of the robust sort. It was not sicklied over with the pale cast of the closet. They could take it with them to the fields, to the slave-pen, the auction-block, wherever they went. This ideal life was aggressively active and not merely defensive from the attacks of Satan; his ramparts must be attacked and taken.

"We want no cowards in our band,
That will their colors fly,
We call for valiant-hearted men,
Who're not afraid to die."

Between Black and White

Or:

"What do you say, seekers,
About that gospel war?"

The Christian life was one of growth; perfection was not gained by a single bound but was a matter of development — a "growing in grace." The old doctrine of the perseverance of the saints crops out in their songs in a very unique way. Seeing the inch-worm measuring his way along slowly on the ground inch by inch, some ingenious slave seized upon this as a symbol of the Christian rate of progress. And is it not so?

"'Twas inch by inch I sought the Lord,
    Jesus will come by an' by,
An' inch by inch he blessed my soul,
    Jesus will come by an' by.

"We'll inch an' inch an' inch along,
    Jesus will come by an' by,
An' inch an' inch till we get home,
    Jesus will come by an' by.

Chorus —
"Keep a-inchin' along, keep a-inchin' along,
    Jesus will come by an' by,
Keep a-inchin' along like the poor inch-worm,
    Jesus will come by an' by."

In this is epitomized the sublime patience of a race for two and a half centuries.

Theology of the Southern Slave Songs

The end of the Christian life was blessedness. Life was a stormy sea. When the other side was reached there would be a new order of things. Sorrow and sighing would flee away. The ills of this life would not disturb there. This is set forth in one of their characteristic songs:

> "No more auction block for me,
>   No more, no more,
>   Many a thousan' gone.
> No more peck o' corn for me,
>   No more, no more,
>   Many a thousan' gone.
> No more pint o' salt for me,
>   No more, no more,
>   Many a thousan' gone.
> No more mistress' call for me,
>   No more, no more,
>   Many a thousan' gone.
> No more driver's lash for me,
>   No more, no more,
>   Many a thousan' gone."

The climax of this Christian life was holiness. There is little evidence that they believed in a state of perfection in this life; in heaven alone no sin would be found. It was theirs to strive for that perfection which practically they might never reach in this world. They strove to be holy:

"Oh, make a-me holy, holy, I do love, I do love;
Make a-me holy, holy; I do love, I do love the Lord."

Between Black and White

Thus we have seen that their conception of the Christian life was that it was a life of development, of activity, of morality, of faith, whose end was blessedness and holiness. Is not this the gist of the Christian conception of life — a life of trust and service, whose end is blessedness?

THE THEOLOGY OF THE SONGS OF THE SOUTHERN SLAVE

(Continued)

CHAPTER VII

The Theology of the Songs of the Southern Slave
(*Continued*)

THEIR BELIEF AS TO SATAN

THE slaves' belief in Satan was positive and strong. For this no doubt they found ample self-evident proofs in themselves and in those with whom they had to do. Their expressions would lead to the belief that they believed in a personal devil — as did Luther! Listen as they sing of their enemy:

"As I went down in the valley to pray,
 I met ole Satan on the way;
 An' what do you think ole Satan say?
 'You're too young to die and too young to pray.' "

They believed that Satan was not only their enemy, not only the arch-enemy of the soul, but also the enemy of all righteousness. In that hymn of hope, "Rise an' shine for the light is comin'," in which they saw the sun of righteousness and liberty rising out of the crimson tide of approaching civil war, they

77

realized that before permanent good could
come to them Satan must be overthrown.

> "We'll build our tent on this camp ground,
> An' pull ole Satan's kingdom down;
> My Lord says he's comin' by an by."

Satan was crafty and deceptive. Like the
writer of the story of the creation they compared him to a serpent — "a snake in the
grass":

> "Ole Satan's like a snake in the grass;
> If you don't mind he'll get you at last."

Full of deception, his was a cloven-foot. His
ever-present hindering and bothering called
forth in one of their songs this frank expression:

> "Why don't the devil let a-me be?"

Does not this forcibly remind us of that remarkable passage of Paul in which he speaks
of the presence of evil when he would do good?

To these untutored minds God stood for all
that was good, Satan for all that was bad.
God was good; the devil was evil. He was
evil and evil continually; out of him could
come no good thing. The principles of these
opposite beings entered the hearts of men;
their lives showed which they served. In the
darkest hour of the night of bondage they

Theology of the Southern Slave Songs

never lost faith in the triumph of right over wrong. The origin of this optimism is not clear unless we conclude that it was revealed to them in their secret communion with God. Untutored, unlettered, as they were, they were yet skilled in the oracles of God, and had much deeper insight into the plans of the Unseen than many who lay claim to an abundance of earthly knowledge. In one of their joyous camp meeting songs they break forth as if by inspiration in this bold prophecy:

"There's a better day a-comin'!
Clap your hands, children."

From their valley of weeping and desolation they beheld the beautiful feet of One upon the mountain tops bringing good tidings of great joy.

THEIR BELIEF AS TO THE FUTURE

To the slave the future life was a necessity — heaven for the reward of the righteous, hell for the wicked. The gaining of heaven and the shunning of hell were the leading motives held out to men to repent. To this doctrine may be traced the element of other worldliness apparent in their songs. It is a common saying among the ex-slaves of the older type: "You may have all the world, just so you give me Jesus." The profitableness of godliness for this life was not so prominent in their belief as was its profitableness for the life to come.

Let us examine their whole system of the future life, beginning with the resurrection. They were not materialists; their bodies were more than those of the lower animals. Their bodies would live again; as Christ had risen so they would rise. A trumpet would sound "to wake the sleeping nations" who would rise "from every graveyard."

> "You may bury me in the East,
> You may bury me in the West,
> But I'll hear the trumpet sound
> In that mornin'."

This was the favorite hymn of the late President Cravath of Fisk University and was sung at his funeral.

The slaves did not believe they were to be disembodied shades floating about in space, but real bodies with "a local habitation and a name."

> "Oh, Lord, these bones of mine,
> Come together in the mornin'."

The golden shoes, the long white robe, the starry crown, these would not be worn by spirits, but by the resurrected and glorified bodies of the redeemed.

They believed that this world would end in

a wreck of matter and a crash of worlds.
Their belief bears striking resemblance to
passages in Peter and Revelation, which no
doubt inspired the following fervid utterances:

"In that great gettin'-up mornin'
Fare you well!   Fare you well!

"The Lord spoke to Gabriel:
  'Say, go look behind the altar,
  Take down the silver trumpet,
  Blow your trumpet, Gabriel.'

" 'Lord, how loud shall I blow it?'
  'Blow it right calm and easy,
  Do not alarm my people,
  Tell them to come to judgment;
  Gabriel, blow your trumpet.'

" 'Lord, how loud shall I blow it?'
  'Loud as seven peals of thunder!
  Wake the sleepin' nations.'

"Then you see poor sinners risin',
  Then you see the world on fire;

"You see the moon a-bleedin',
  See the stars a-fallin',
  See the elements meltin',
  See the forked lightnin',
  Hear the thunder rumblin';
  Earth shall reel and totter.

Between Black and White

"Then you see the Christian risin',
Then you see the righteous marchin',
They are marchin' home to heaven.
Then you see my Jesus comin'
With all his holy angels,
Take the righteous home to heaven,
There they live with God forever."

They believed in the general judgment, for which all were exhorted to get ready:

"Judgment day is a-rollin' around;
Judgment! Judgment!
Oh, how I long to go!"

The issues of the judgment were everlasting punishment and everlasting happiness. It was ill with the wicked and well with the good. A beautiful melody was built up on the parable of the virgins, showing the different results of the judgment for the wise and the foolish. That they believed in future punishment, severe and endless, seems strange. "It would seem as if this whole race of Lazaruses," says one, "who received only the crumbs as they fell from the rich tables of the masters, would feel that they had experienced their full share of trouble in this life. But no! they firmly held to the idea that sin must be punished, and incorporated this idea in their songs." The following is a good sample from one of many illustrating this point:

82

Theology of the Southern Slave Songs

"My Lord, what a mornin'
When the stars begin to fall;
You'll hear the sinner moan,
When the stars begin to fall."

But while their belief in future punishment
was vivid their hope for the blessings be-
stowed by the heavenly Father was bright
and fadeless. Observe the ring of certitude
with which they sang:

"The man who loves to serve the Lord,
When death shall shake this frame,
He shall receive his just reward,
When death shall shake this frame."

The impromptu lyrics of the slave poets
were at their best when depicting the glories
of the happy land. Allowed entrance to their
master's mansion only by the back way and
as servants, their hearts kindled at the pros-
pect of an abundant entrance to the heavenly
mansion. They forgot the miserable cabins
in which they lived when they sang:

"In bright mansions above,
In bright mansions above,
Lord, I want to live up yonder,
In bright mansions above."

Misery was their lot here, but:

"Wait a little while, then
We'll sing the new song,
Wait a little while;

83

Between Black and White

> My heavenly home is bright an' fair,
> We will sing the new song;
> No pain nor sorrow enters there,
> Then we'll sing the new song."

There were angels waiting at the door to convey the faithful to the land of happiness.

The hope of immortality is prominent in these songs. Was there ever a Negro slave who did not believe in God? in heaven? in immortality? The grave was not life's goal; there was a life beyond unmeasured by the flight of years; there death was not known. God would

> "Take the righteous home to heaven,
> There they'll live with him forever."

Remarkable as are these songs for what they contain, they are still more remarkable for what they do not contain. In the first place, their conceptions are orthodox. Doubtless they heard unorthodox preaching, but that none of this is manifest in their songs shows that it requires truth to inspire the genuinely religious heart. In their songs we find the essentials of Christianity dwelt upon, while the non-essentials are conspicuously absent. Many slaves had Roman Catholic masters, especially in Louisiana. It was the custom in the slave states for the slave, if he attended religious services, to attend the same ones that his master did. We may be assured that not a few slaves received Roman Catholic indoctrination. But strange to say these songs are free from Mariolatry. As far as I can discover by research and experience I find no melody of the slave singing divine praises to the Virgin.

Again, we observe the entire absence of the spirit of revenge in these songs, which comprised their whole public utterance. To read, to write, to make public address, these were denied the slave. Ignorance was the corner stone of slavery. Hence they sang their thoughts. Human nature must have an expression. Although these songs comprised, as I have said, the whole public utterance of a people for two and a half centuries, yet there cannot be found in them a single trace of ill will! Does the world present a parallel to this? Compare this with the Psalms. David, oppressed by his enemies, called down fire, hail, and burning wind, to consume them from the very face of the earth. But no such speech as that ever fell from the lips of the typical American slave. He rested his case with God, to whom belongeth vengeance. The Judge of all the earth would do right. When public prejudice shall have passed away and the future historian shall write unbiased by race feeling

he will dip his pen in the clear sunlight of
justice and catalogue this among the virtues
of the American slave. Coming generations
will read with admiring wonder of this oppressed people who so forcibly remind one of
Him who was oppressed, yet humbled himself and opened not his mouth.

Thus we have found in our survey of these
songs that the conceptions of God, of Christ,
of the Holy Spirit, of the angels, of Satan,
of the Christian life, and of the future are
orthodox, and that there is a remarkable
absence of certain heretical and vindictive
elements which naturally they might be supposed to contain.

What is the origin of these conceptions?
The slaves, as I have before stated, always
had the privilege of attending the religious
services of their masters. At certain periods
they were allowed services of their own at
which a white minister presided. In some
families provision was made for special religious instruction, limited in scope and
character, for the slaves. Occasionally there
were services for and by the slaves. In these
meetings their songs were perfected. In the
other meetings they got their material; mean-
while, at their daily tasks, it was worked over
in their minds. When they came to their
own meetings, wrought upon by a deep re-

ligious enthusiasm, they gave vent to their feelings in expressions of burning rhythmic utterances of soul-stirring song. Thus were these unique songs conceived and born.

Such a tenacious grasp of the fundamental and essential truths of Christianity by these unlettered slaves in the midst of social confusion and moral error is indicative of the original qualities of mind and heart of the Negro people, and is calculated to inspire with renewed hope those who have so earnestly wrought and confidently longed for the evangelization of the black man both in America and Africa.

THE LURE OF THE NEW SOUTH

CHAPTER VIII

The Lure of the New South

ON the day of my graduation Professor Stevens, who later visited my church in Atlanta, came to me and said: "You are now prepared to fill any pulpit in the land." I appreciated his kind expression. But my heart was in the Southland, and I was happy to respond to the call of the First Congregational Church of Atlanta immediately upon my graduation, where I had the privilege of serving as minister for a quarter of a century. I reached Atlanta on Memorial Day, and began my work in this central city of the new South at the most inspiring time of the year in the beautiful Southland.

The South is the most unique part of our country. With its rare climate, remarkable fertility, romantic history, and baffling racial atmosphere, it holds a fascination no other part of our country does. But its greatest charm for me at the time was that it was the chief home of the people of whom I was a part, and I longed to go back and help them. It was, therefore, with peculiar pleasure that I turned my face toward the South when I had finished my study at Yale. I went from

Between Black and White

New England to the new South to put into practice some of the things I had been nurturing in my heart all my lifetime.

In the sense that Paris is France, London, England, and New York, America, so is Atlanta the South. Atlanta is a unique city sitting on more hills than ancient Rome. It is too near the stars for a flood, being a thousand feet above the level of the sea. It has one of the most ideal climates of any city in the United States. It is the commercial center of the Southeast. There she sits like a goddess, with one hand on the coffers of the East and the other on the products of the South. Every great business house in the country has a sub-office in Atlanta, so that the city has more skyscrapers than any other city of its size in the world. And I have sometimes said that Atlanta is the biggest city of its size in America!

Atlanta has more colleges for colored youth than any other city in the world. On one hill stands Atlanta University, founded by the Congregationalists; on another Atlanta Baptist College, a school for young men; on another Spelman Seminary, a Baptist school for girls (named for Mrs. Rockefeller); on another Clark University, founded by the Methodists; on another Gammon Theological Seminary, a theological school endowed by

The Lure of the New South

the Methodists with a million dollars; and on still another Morris Brown College, founded by the African Methodists (a monument to self-help and sacrifice). The encircling hills of Atlanta are crowned with colleges for colored youth like bonfires of living light. And these very hills were once occupied by contending armies, for Atlanta is built on a battlefield. It was here that Sherman broke the backbone of the rebellion. It was in this city that Sherman gave his famous definition of war. It was here that the famous march to the sea began.

In the very heart of this city, within a block of where the first shell of the battle of Atlanta struck, killing a little child, is located the First Congregational Church of Atlanta. This church was organized one year before I was born. Its first ministers came from New England, and were graduates of Yale. They organized the Storrs School, the first school in Georgia for colored people, and in this school the church was born. This church in turn became the mother of Atlanta University. This may account for the fact that so large a proportion of its members are imbued with the spirit of education.

It was to this church, housed in a little brick structure on the corner, that I was called. The membership was composed of some of the finest people in Atlanta. The only fault I found with them was that there were not enough of them. I preached on quality plus quantity, and the one hundred members grew to two hundred, three hundred, and on up to a thousand. In its growth the quality was preserved.

This church had some remarkable characteristics. In it was organized the first temperance society in Georgia, and its members were required to sign a pledge of total abstinence for admission. It thus became the forerunner of prohibition in Georgia, the South, and the nation. From the beginning the spirit of thrift was instilled in its members, and today two-thirds of them own their own homes; some of these are among the most beautiful and commodious in the city. Industry was one of the things instilled in the early day, and today you cannot find the name of a loafer on the church roll. As a matter of fact, just being a member of that church is sufficient as a credential for employment. Great stress was laid on putting religion into character, so that in all the history of the church only one man was ever sent to the state prison, and not a single one was ever accused of the unspeakable crime against womanhood. The death rate in the church was lower than that among the white popula-

tion by one third. Of the thousand members
of the church not one was illiterate.

In this church was organized the National
Convention of Congregational Workers
Among the Colored People by Dr. George W.
Henderson, professor at Straight University,
New Orleans, Louisiana, and myself, through
the inspiration of the Young People's Congress, which brought together young colored
people from all parts of the country. The
purpose of this convention was to bring together for mutual helpfulness the workers in
church and school in the Congregational
churches of the colored people. The first
meeting of the organization was held in Atlanta, the next in New Orleans, and the third
in Memphis, meeting once in two years.
This organization has grown year by year
until it is the most hopeful thing among the
colored Congregational churches in the United
States.

It was while attending the meeting of this
convention at Memphis that tidings came to
me of the breaking out of the Atlanta Riot,
Saturday, Sept. 22, 1906. It can be easily
imagined how distressing was the news when
it is recalled that not only were my church
people there, but also my children left in the
care of a friend. The papers contained increasingly unfavorable reports of conditions,

and we hastened home, only to find the city in two hostile camps, with the blood of both races undried on the streets of the city. Fortunately our children were safe, although rioters came into the church yard and looked into the windows of the church, while my children looked out through the shutters of the parsonage near by. Although many were killed and wounded, not a member of my church was hurt. But my heart went out beyond the members of my parish, and I endeavored to console all I could.

While on this errand of mercy a surprising call came to me from a lawyer in the city. His name was Charles T. Hopkins, a native-born Southerner trained in an Eastern institution. We bared our hearts on the situation, and felt that something must be done and that we were the ones to do it. A plan was agreed upon, and he called in two white men and I called in two colored men. These six agreed, and a still larger number were called in, making twenty on each side. Through these two bodies working together peace was restored. It was found that both working together could do things that neither group could do alone. This was the beginning of the movement for interracial cooperation in the South. Other cities adopted the plan, and now there is a permanent organiza-

The Lure of the New South

tion working on this line with headquarters
in Atlanta and New York. Without doubt
this is the key to the solution of the problem
of the races not only in the South, but also
in the North, and in all the world where white
and colored races meet in large numbers.

My efforts in this line were not without
much misunderstanding and actual danger.
Some among my own people felt that I was
giving away their case by seeking cooperation
with the whites. Others thought that because I had openly denounced the conditions
productive of riots that I had therefore produced the riot. Only a week before the riot
I had spoken before the city council, saying
that unless they closed up the dives of the
city blood would run in the streets. In response to my plea the city council passed an
ordinance closing the dives, but it was too
late; the poison was in the blood. Through
misrepresentation in the press false rumors
were started, and on Saturday night the
crowds that poured in from the surrounding
towns for a frolic were stampeded into the
bloody riot that followed and upset the city
for a week.

During the upset conditions that followed,
my name was much in the mouths of the
people because of the part I took in attempt-
ing to promote peace. One evening near

97

dusk a colored man came to my front porch with a bludgeon in his hand, and called for me. Fortunately, my wife met him at the door, and when that good woman looked him in the eyes he tucked his head and ran. I was in the little parlor within a few feet of him, but did not know of the nature of his errand until after he had gone.

Not long after, another queer character came to see me. Again, my wife let him in. She informed me of his presence, but said she did not like his looks. But I went right in to see him, and I met a typical Georgia Cracker. His hair was long and dishevelled, his elbows protruded through his sleeves, and he made a most formidable appearance. As I entered he quickly rose from his chair, and took me by both my hands, saying, "My dear brother, I have followed your course in the matter of the riot. I sympathize with you. I love your people, and I have come to pray with you." We fell on our knees and prayed together. I have heard the great metropolitan preachers pray, but no prayer ever touched my heart like the prayer of this plain man from the backwoods of Georgia. I never saw him before, and I have never seen him since. His going and coming were like that of Elijah.

But after the storm came the calm, and we

98

looked up and saw the rainbow covering the
shoulder of the dying storm. In that hour
God gave me a message for my people. It
was only natural that they should want to
leave. I tried to assure them that out of
this would come a better Atlanta, that now
was the time to settle down and build anew.
That voice was heeded, for few left the city.
Some of those who did leave came back later.
The breaches were healed, the work of cooperation between the better elements of
both races progressed, and it was the unanimous opinion that the city was better afterwards than before.

But in order to make this appeal effective
I had to produce some tangible evidence to
my people that the good will of them was
genuine. In that hour a vision came to me.
For ten years I had sat on my porch near the
church and seen the people of my race go by
the church down to the dive, into the prison,
up to the gallows. I asked myself why it was
that the people passed by my church and
went to the dive. The answer was simple.
My church was locked and barred and dark,
while the dive was wide open, illuminated,
and attractive. Then I said: "God helping
me, I will open my church and make it as
attractive as the dive."

To do this required money. My people

were not rich, and had many obligations. In response to my appeal they subscribed ten thousand dollars. Colored people of other denominations subscribed two and a half thousand dollars. I made an appeal to the white people for a similar amount and they gave twice as much, thus demonstrating their good will. I then turned to the people of the North on the ground that this was a national question, and that this was a good way to promote interracial good will. My appeal made in many churches throughout the North was generously responded to, and the funds came to make real the vision I had seen. Of the realization of this vision I will speak more fully later.

One who rendered invaluable service in the work I undertook was Booker T. Washington. I first met him when he came to Atlanta to deliver the speech at the Cotton States Exposition that made him famous. I sat beside his wife as he leaped into fame. Afterwards he frequently came to my church to speak, and was often a guest in my home. I had the privilege annually of securing large audiences for him to speak to in our city auditorium. In turn he was of much help to my cause. It was through him that the Ogden party came to our church one Sunday on their way to Tuskegee, and made our church the center

of the city for the day. This gave me an introduction to some of the leading people in
the North, and greatly helped me in securing
funds for my larger work. Mr. Washington
was also generous in giving me the names of
influential people, and he presented me once
before the Twentieth Century Club of Boston. I found his name a key North and
South. I once called upon Mr. Carnegie in
New York to give a portion to my organ
fund, and he asked me whom I had to recom-
mend me, and I told him I had letters from
ex-President Roosevelt, President Taft, Sena-
tor Smith, and Booker T. Washington. He
said that if I had the recommendation of Mr.
Washington I did not need the others. I left
off the names of the others, and I got my
request.

As is well known, there are two wings to
the colored race, the radical and the conservative. The more radical is headed by Dr.
W. E. B. DuBois, and the conservative by
Dr. Washington. I was in school with Mr.
DuBois and I have worked most harmoniously
with Mr. Washington. I was a friend to
both, and I believe there is much good in the
positions of both. But there need be no
conflict. They are the right and left wings
of a great movement. Just as a bird must
have both wings for successful flight, so

101

163132

must any movement have the radical and
conservative wings. I can recall when Dr.
Washington and Dr. DuBois worked together
harmoniously. Many a time have they come
to my house, sometimes in the night, and we
have conferred together on plans that were
afterwards consummated. The same position I took then I take now. If there is any
one thing my people need it is that broadness
of spirit by which the radical and conservative elements may work together unitedly for
the advancement of the race as a whole.
This spirit of cooperation, not only between
the various wings of the race but also between
white and black, was perhaps the chief contribution the First Church of Atlanta made
to social betterment during the quarter of a
century of my pastorate.

THE BELLS OF ATLANTA

CHAPTER IX

The Bells of Atlanta

I ONCE overheard a hot-blooded young white Southerner say that the race question would be settled at the point of the bayonet and by the shedding of blood. The question will be settled by sword and blood, but it will be by the sword of the spirit and the blood of the Lamb. My invariable answer to the oft-asked question as to whether there will be a race war in the South is in the negative. I base this opinion on the overlooked fact that both races in the South are religious. Our white people are religious; they keep the Sabbath, they go to church, and they read their Bibles. In fact, they form the very backbone of American orthodoxy. We colored people are nothing if not religious. We have a genius for religion, and it is not too much to say that we are the most religious people in the world.

When I first went to Niagara I saw a beautiful body of water going over a precipice a mile wide. It was a magnificent sight, but power was going to waste. When I went there again some shrewd Yankee had hitched those falls to a dynamo, by which they made

enough electricity to light up the whole re-
gion for many miles around. There runs in
the South a magnificent stream of religion, to
which both races contribute, but too much of
it is going to waste. The religion of the South
is sentimental rather than practical, individual
rather than social. Hitch up the religion of
the South to its great unsolved problem, and
a new day will come to that section.

That was the vision that came to me in the
midst of my ministry in the South, and we
endeavored to hitch up the First Church of
Atlanta to the great problem of the South.
The first step in this direction was to secure a
church building adapted for the purpose.
The result was the structure that now stands
in the heart of the city. I saw this building
rise from the foundation to the capstone, and
much of my life is built into its very walls.
There is a basement, containing Sunday-
school facilities, a library and a reading room,
a gymnasium, a kitchen, a shower bath, the
engine room, and lavatories. On the main
floor is an auditorium with a seating capacity
of one thousand. Here are also the office of
the church and the study of the pastor. On
the third floor are a gallery and a ladies'
parlor. In this industrial temple we dedi-
cated the pulpit and the parlor, the auditorium and the organ, the dumb-bell and the

First Congregational Church, Atlanta, Georgia
Erected under leadership of Henry Hugh. Proctor

needle, the skillet and the tub, to the glory of God and the redemption of a race.

Hard by the church stood the parsonage, next to which was the home for colored working girls. This was the first home in the world opened by any church for colored girls. The colored girl is the most unprotected woman in all the world, and it was an inspiring occasion when the home was opened for service to this needy group. This was the best equipped church plant for colored people anywhere in the world, and is conservatively estimated to be worth $250,000.

At the time it was opened it met in each of its facilities a special need. There was no Y. M. C. A. for colored young men in the city, and ours was the only gymnasium in the city for that group. There was no Y. W. C. A. in the city, and our home for young colored women was the only one of its kind in Atlanta. There was an employment bureau, and in this we served the people of both races in the city. A water fountain outside the church (breaking the color line) was the first water fountain opened in the city. Our trouble bureau was a clinic for all sorts of ills. Our prison mission served the man at the very bottom. Our Music Festival brought the best musical talent of the race to the city, and attracted great audiences of both races. As a matter of fact, we found that music was a great solvent of racial antipathies, just as David found it a solvent for personal antagonism with Saul.

These facilities were at the disposal of all, Monday as well as Sunday, night as well as day. We served all without regard to denominational or racial affiliation. It was in the real sense a church of the people. Its purpose was to serve man in his threefold nature, body, mind, and spirit. It will be remembered that the great Founder of the church went about teaching, the ministry to the mind; preaching, the ministry to the spirit; and healing, the ministry to the body. I predict that when the church catches up with Jesus she will again exert her old-time power, not in the old way, but in a new and better way. It will do better than merely save men's souls; it will save the whole man, body, mind, and soul. Save the body alone, and you have a Jack Johnson; save the mind alone, and you have a Robert Ingersoll; save the soul alone, and you have an Uncle Tom; but save body, mind, and soul, and you have an Apostle Paul — a Jesus Christ!

Naturally such a church with such a program began to attract attention. It was doing things. Visitors came from all parts of the world. Among these were many newspaper writers. Dr. Abbott, of the *Outlook*, came, and because of its Circles of Ten, an original form of church work, called it the best organized church in the South. Bruce Barton spent a Sunday with us, and after studying the work of the church in the Atlanta Riot called it "The Church That Saved a City," in a brilliant article published in *The Congregationalist and Christian World*. One of the shrewdest observers that visited us was Russell Conwell, who after looking through the building examined the doorstep, to see how it was worn, and it passed the test.

But we were honored with the presence of two men who had sat in the presidential chair at Washington. The first was Mr. Taft, who just before his inauguration visited the South, and in coming to Atlanta was shown our church by his millionaire host as one of the sights of the city. He and I were photographed together on the front steps of the church, and the photograph was sent throughout the country. As he stood there the choir sang in his honor the Negro melody, "Let Us Cheer the Weary Traveler." I revisited my old church some time ago, and was greatly delighted that they sang this selection for me. It became our custom to sing this melody for those visitors we wanted especially to honor. We were greatly impressed

Between Black and White

with the big-heartedness of Mr. Taft as he
went about in the building patting little children on the head.

The other was Mr. Roosevelt, who came to
us just after his return from Africa. I shall
never forget the first question he asked as he
entered the church radiating enthusiasm.
After he had signed his name in big, bold
hand on the church register, he turned upon
me sharply and said: "Mr. Proctor, what is
an institutional church?" I had supposed
that he knew everything. "Come with me,
Mr. Roosevelt," I replied, "and I will show
you." First I took him to the reading room,
and on the table among other periodicals was
the *Outlook* — "Theodore Roosevelt, Con-
tributing Editor." "You understand that,
Mr. Roosevelt," I said. "Delighted," he replied. Then I took him to the gymnasium,
with its dumb-bells, riding-horse, etc. "You
understand that," I said. "Bully, bully!" he
exclaimed. Then I took him into the kitchen,
named in honor of my mother, and he inquired if we could make real cooks there.
When I told him we could, he expressed very
great satisfaction. Then I took him to the
men's room of the church, named in his
honor, and in which hung a picture of himself, above which was poised a big stick.
This pleased him greatly, and he chuckled

delightedly. When he came into the main
auditorium, where he was greeted by a great
audience, he made a notable address. Among
other things, he said that he hailed the day
when churches like this were opened, churches
that served all the people. Later, when I
saw him in New York City, he presented me
to Father John, telling him how he was impressed with the First Church of Atlanta.

Of course, other churches began to do the
same thing. Imitation is the sincerest form
of flattery. One of the most notable instances of this is the St. John's Church,
Springfield, Mass., which, under the inspiring
leadership of Dr. W. N. DeBerry, has im-
proved on the original conception by our
church. Another instance is that of the
Tabernacle Baptist Church of Augusta, of
which the late Rev. C. T. Walker was builder.
Another church was built on this plan in
Harlem, the largest Negro city in the world.
The present condition of the colored people
demands this type of church for their full
development.

Congregationalism has to its credit the ini-
tiation of many forward movements. Among
these are the emancipation of the slave, the
education of the freedmen, the temperance
movement, the evangelistic movement, and
the Young People's Society of Christian En-

Between Black and White

deavor. To this might be added the social service movement among the colored churches. This type of church polity, with its freedom from formalism, lends itself readily to the movement for reform, and would be of very great advantage to the colored people generally. They have been so long used to bondage that they are heartily fond of freedom. It is not surprising, therefore, that there is a movement in the West among the colored people in Episcopally governed churches toward Congregationalism. To congregationalize the Negro would be to solve his problem as far as he himself could do it. That was the verdict passed upon the colored people congregationalized in Atlanta. One of the things I learned from President Cravath at Fisk was so to live that prejudice against one would be unreasonable. While at Yale I endeavored so to act that the only fault that could be found of me was my color, and I am happy to say I heard of no fault found with that. I believe this is the secret for my people to solve their problem, which, after all, is much simpler than most of us have imagined.

At the National Council of Congregational Churches held at Des Moines, Iowa, I was chosen assistant moderator of the Council by unanimous vote of the body. This was the

112

greatest honor that had ever come to me, and I think it came in recognition of my efforts as peace-maker in the Atlanta Riot. I shall always be grateful to Dr. Amory H. Bradford, of Montclair, N. J., for nominating me for this position. It gave me great encouragement in the work I was endeavoring to do for my people, and I think the incident proved helpful to my people as a whole. Later, I had the opportunity of preaching in Dr. Bradford's great church at Montclair. It was during his last days, and his frail body was shaking like a reed. As he introduced me as I stood by his side, he exclaimed: "Oh, that I had this man's body," and I turned to him and said: "Oh, that I had this man's brain!" He was one of the greatest, wisest, and most courageous friends my people ever had, and that is saying a great deal.

But my greatest joy in Atlanta was to see my people grow in the things that were worth while. It was a pleasure to see the children grow into men and women of influence and power. That joy was increased when I began to baptize the children of those whom I had myself consecrated to the service of the Master. Today I cannot go into any part of the country that I do not find some of the people I had the privilege of training in spiritual things. The best church member I ever knew was a woman in this church. She joined the whole church, and attended every meeting. She gave to everything, and was a peace-maker among the people. At one time she gave the church $200, and at another time $500, for which she washed with her own hands. There were in the church over a hundred college graduates, but it was the unanimous opinion that she had a certain culture none of these graduates could claim. It was the culture of the Spirit. Her loyalty and fidelity never wavered for a quarter of a century. She is the best church member I ever knew. It was a privilege in a recent Western journey to be under her roof just for a night, and to recall the days when we walked in tune with the bells of Atlanta.

IN TRIBUTE TO THE GENEROUS

CHAPTER X

In Tribute to the Generous

I NEVER begged a dollar in my life. But, what is a very different thing, I have had the opportunity of leading some people to invest in good causes. The one is degrading and humiliating; the other is ennobling.

In this work of getting others to invest in good causes I have incurred scars in my heart of which I have never told anyone, and in these pages I shall preserve a similar reticence. On the other hand, this work has produced some of the most inspiring experiences of my life. Of these I wish to speak here.

One of the greatest opportunities that can come to anyone is that of building a church. It seems to me that in such an experience come revelations of life such as can come in no other way. I can never forget the experiences I had in the building of the First Church of Atlanta. In this work I had the opportunity of leading many people to help a most worthy cause.

The first to whom I turned for help were

117

the members of the church themselves. Frankly, many of them felt that the task was impossible, and they plainly said so. In fact, some thought I was going crazy. On the other hand, the vast majority had faith that it could be done, and they subscribed with a liberal hand. I recall that one man, a classmate of Booker T. Washington, pledged $250; and when he heard some others say that it could not be done, showed his faith in the project by drawing a check for the whole sum. I cannot tell how much sentiment this prompt action turned in favor of the movement. One woman subscribed $500, and the next week she paid the amount in full, handing to our treasurer one hundred crisp five-dollar bills. I can see those beautiful fresh bank notes now.

After the members had subscribed ten thousand dollars, I turned to the other colored people of the community with the plea that this was to be a community church, and as such, would help every man and woman of our race in the city. Many felt that in view of the intense denominational feeling there would be no response. But I have learned to trust human nature, and we were gratified with the gift of $2,500 from colored people of other denominations. This served to break down much sectarian feeling, and give the whole colored population a real interest and a sense of possession in the church.

Although at this time the experiences of the riot were in the minds of the people, we turned to the white people of Atlanta, asking them to give $2,500. Many of the pessimists among my own people declared that it was idle to ask for such an amount. But after a week of personal canvassing I came back with $5,000 in cold, hard cash. In this canvass I did not encounter a single discourtesy. I have never raised any money from any group of people that gave me greater pleasure.

I recall going to one man, a certain bishop, and asking him for the names of men to whom I might appeal. He gave me the name of every man except the one I had hoped he would. I finally took courage to ask about that particular man, and I was informed that he could not give me a dollar in view of the fact that he was doing so many things already. I left the bishop, got on the cars, and went as direct to that brother as I could go. I found him alone and straightway broached the object of my call. In response, he told me that every dollar he had belonged to the Lord; and then he added, "Your work seems to be the Lord's work and I will give you what you ask." I asked him for only $100. I learned my lesson, however, and on another occasion I asked him for $3,000 and got it! On another occasion I called on a man who had the reputation of being the meanest man in town. (I have found out that such men contribute more readily because many people are afraid of them and as a result they are not bothered so much.) I stated my case, and to my surprise he said: "Talk about political equality, intellectual equality, and social equality; they are all in the Christian spirit. Just lift your people up, and they will get everything coming to them. Here is $100 to help you do it." May I here record that in the quarter of a century I was in Atlanta I never attempted a good thing for my people but that I found some Southern white man by my side helping me do it.

One of the things that greatly helped me in this appeal, as well as in other things I attempted to do in a public way, was the courtesy of the press. They never failed to give due publicity to any matter I wanted to get before the public. The Altanta Constitution, the Georgia Bible, weekly printed excerpts from my sermons for a number of years. Once they printed my sermon in full on the first page. The paper did this in the face of opposition from some quarters. The city editor once showed me a letter from a white minister making complaint because my sermon was printed next to his. At that time an entire page in the Monday edition was given to sermons. After that they scattered the sermons through the paper as news, and I noted that this minister's sermons were conspicuous by their absence. Of course, this aroused jealousy among some of my own people, and I was accused of possible disloyalty to my own race, but the charge fell flat because they could not point to a single disloyal word. None knew better the falsity of this charge than the white people themselves with whom I always dealt in a frank and courteous manner.

With this beginning among the people of Atlanta I turned to the people of the North. I had spoken on various occasions in Northern cities, and had entertained the Ogden Party in Atlanta, so that I was pretty well acquainted with the generous people of the North. At this time an incident occurred that seemed at first untoward, but turned out greatly to my advantage. I was addressing the National Council of Congregational Churches in Cleveland, Ohio, and in this address I planned to make an appeal .to the churches of the North for cooperation in the work of building the institutional church in Atlanta. In opening I indulged in some humorous allusions, and spent more time in getting started than I had suspected. Scarcely had I gotten to the nub of the matter before the presiding officer called time on me. And although the house clamored for me to proceed, he was obdurate in view of the fact that a funeral was to be held in the building at a certain hour. Crestfallen, I took my seat, thinking I had sustained an irreparable loss. But at the close of the meeting many came to me and said they were anxious to hear all I had to say. I told them that I would come to their church, and give them the rest of the speech. This opened the door for the hearing to get the money I needed. Since that day, when I have had a door shut in my face, I look for the open door and I have never failed to find it.

I can never be sufficiently grateful to the people of the North for the kind and generous reception they gave me in this campaign in church, home, and office. In the beginning of the campaign there occurred an incident for which I shall ever be grateful. I called to see a man in Chicago who told me that he had no money for me but that he could tell me how to get it. I replied that that would be of more value than any material gift he could make. He then told me how he had collected many thousands of dollars for good causes on the principle. It was this: he never asked a man for money without prayer. When he approached the building in which that man was located he would enter with prayer; and when he reached the person, he would be praying secretly all the time he was talking to him. I shall ever be grateful for this method. It is the secret of all the money I have received for good causes, and I regard every penny I get an answer to prayer. But of course this does not mean that I believe in faith without works; I believe in faith with works.

It was always a pleasure to deal with women. I remember speaking in a church in Connecticut, and observing in the audience a woman who seemed greatly interested. I called to see her the next day, and was quietly received by her. She assured me of her interest in my work, saying that I would hear from her later. I was delighted one morning to receive a letter addressed in a feminine hand with a check for $500. This was not her last time to give.

I remember calling to see another good woman in Connecticut and telling her of my work. She was an invalid and unable to leave her home, and was, therefore, hungry for spiritual fellowship. After I had stated my mission, she consented to give me $100. I asked permission to sing her one of the songs of my people. When I had finished she volunteered to double the amount, assuring me she would send the check the next day. When the check came it was for $300.

There was one good woman with whom I failed signally She was afflicted with deafness, and could only hear by the use of a speaking trumpet. I would tell my story, and the moment I approached the business end she would lower the trumpet. I made the attack again and again with like result, finally retiring in amusement. She won. I charge that to the shrewdness of Boston.

It was in a western town that a woman once saved me. I had spoken in the church, and was making the rounds of the generous the next day. I went to a certain home, and on meeting the man of the house at the door, he hesitated to admit me on the ground that he did not know me. While I was endeavoring to tell him who I was, a lady in the rear heard my voice and came to my relief. She was a teacher I had known at Fisk many years ago. After an introduction my expectation was rewarded.

On another occasion I called to see a generous lady and, after stating my errand, I was about to specify to her the amount I wanted, as I found out by experience that people liked to have you do that. I had my

mouth open endeavoring to ask her for $100,
when she announced, not perceiving what I
was about to say, that she could give me only
$300! It almost took my breath, and I had
difficulty in getting my mouth shut grace-
fully.

But I am equally grateful to the men. I
shall ever be grateful to Dr. Charles H.
Richards, Secretary of the Congregational
Church Building Society, who not only gave
me introduction to many generous people,
but also secured a generous gift and loan from
his society, without which we could not have
put the matter over. He took a personal interest, came to our church at the time of its
dedication, and gave a noble sermon. I have
sometimes spoken of him as my father in
"white." *

In a certain little city in Massachusetts,
there were three brothers whose generosity
always put me to shame. Once they were
assured of my cause they never hesitated to
give. Their offices were in the same building
and on the same floor. The moment I entered
the office of the elder one he would begin to
write out a check for $100, and by the time I
was seated he would have it ready to hand
me. I would take this to the office of the

* Since these lines were written, Dr. Richards has fallen on sleep, but not
before showing similar interest in my present project.

others, and they would follow suit. A sister would give one-fourth that amount. As a result I would complete my errand there in fifteen minutes.

Among the best people to solicit were those who had the custom of tithing. I recall speaking to a very small audience one stormy night in a little city near Boston. Before I spoke I had sized up the response in my mind, but I decided to do my best. I noticed as I proceeded a man and his wife who seemed deeply interested, and sometimes affected, in my story. At the close of my address they sent a note requesting me to call at the office on the morrow. I asked the minister of the church who this man was. He said that he did not know him very well but was sure he was not a man of any means, and that he would advise me to go back to Boston. Despite this I remained and went to see the man in his office. After telling me of his impressions of my appeal, he said that it was his custom to give one-tenth of his income to good causes, and that he and his wife had decided to give me $100.

He gave half of this in cash, and promised to send the other at a certain time. At the exact time mentioned a check for the balance was received. I want here to bear testimony to my joy in the fidelity with which many

In Tribute to the Generous

such obligations were met. Time and time
again my mail would bring letters bearing
checks on the exact date promised. I lift my
hat to the promptness and reliability of New
England.

I was deeply touched in a Boston bank one
day when a man handed me a gift for my
work. I thanked him for his generosity, but
he waved me aside saying: "You are giving
more than I. I give you a few dollars. You
are giving your life. I thank you." In that
hour I got a new revelation of the motive in
which many give.

But my most generous giver was the late
Ralph Miner of New Haven. I learned that
he and his good wife, who is with us still, had
put a colored lad through school, and that
they had once taught in a colored Sunday-
school. He had also been in the army and
fought for the Union. He had never failed
to make a contribution to my cause when I
called upon him. Finally, I offered to name
all our institutional facilities after him. In
his modesty he hesitated, but urged by Mrs.
Miner, he finally consented. Today the institutional facilities of the First Church of
Atlanta are grouped under his name, and are
known as the Ralph Miner Institute. Mr.
Miner's interest became deepened in our work,
and to the end of his life he regarded himself

my silent partner. If at any time I came short in a campaign he always made up the deficit, and gladly. Once he gave a Ford car that the pastor might make his rounds among his people more comfortably, and that the pastor's wife might have the opportunity of outings. At his death he remembered the Institute in his will. But he left his name indelibly stamped on the hearts of the people of Atlanta, and they rise up to call him blessed.

No gift I received made a deeper impression on me than that of a man in Hartford. I had spoken in Center Church, and among those who greeted me at the close of my talk was a man with a distinctive touch in his grip. The next day I called to see him, and asked the reason. He told me this story: "Sometime ago I was traveling between Birmingham and Atlanta. The train on which I was riding was late, and making up time. Instinctively, I felt that something was going to happen. All at once there was a wild screech of the engine, and the train came to a dead standstill. The conductor got off to see what the matter was. When he returned he said that there was a work train ahead, and in order that we might not run into it a flagman had to come back and stand in the center of the track. We have just picked up

the body of that flagman after our train had
passed over him.   And he was a black man!''

Then I understood the pressure of the hand
and the tear in the eye with which his gift
was accompanied.   This is not the first time
the black man has stood in the middle of the
track to save the lives of others in this land.
He has cleared the fields, spanned the streams
with bridges, built highways, and fought in
every war.   He has done what he could.
Those who receive gifts for the uplift of their
people are ennobled to think that they may
be acting as a medium for the expression of
a gratitude that is deep and genuine.

TRAVELING THROUGH AMERICA
FIRST

CHAPTER XI

Traveling Through America First

THE day I got my first glimpse of the little city of Fayetteville I learned that there was a larger world, and I had a quenchless desire to see it. Fortunately, the opportunity has come to travel far and wide. Errands of study, speaking, and business have called me over a large part of the civilized world. I am glad of an opportunity to have seen America first.

I recall my first visit to New York City. Having lived in a country town all my lifetime, I could not readily grasp the change in the way of doing things necessitated by living in the larger cities. Reaching the wharf of the crowded metropolis, my grip was taken by one I supposed to be a porter for the Grand Union Hotel. He soon had me in a cab which I supposed was free. Pretty soon a second man came out from the sidewalk and demanded my fare of $2.50. When I demurred he threatened to call the police. We finally compromised on $1.00, and then he showed me a street-car that put me at my destination for five cents. That was the most

133

useful dollar I ever spent. It taught me the habit never to let a person do anything for me without first finding out the cost. Although I have traveled many thousands of miles since that day at home and abroad, I cannot recall having been cheated out of another penny.

What a big, busy place I found New York to be! What high buildings, what throngs on Broadway, what a crush at Brooklyn Bridge, where everybody seemed to get up and rush for the entrance at the same time! Here for the first time I heard Talmage, then at the height of his fame. I had read his sermons ever since I was a boy, and I was eager to see him in action. The big church was thronged. There was no choir, but the singing was led by a trumpeter and everybody sang. The famous Brooklyn divine filled the great platform, pacing and racing from side to side. His voice was harsh, however, and I concluded that I had rather read him than hear him.

After a few days spent in the metropolis I was tired and confused, and I rejoiced in the rest and quiet of the boat on the Sound as it bore me from New York to New Haven, where in the gray of the early morning I got my first glimpse of the classic walls of Yale.

Traveling Through America First

There I spent three years, and had the opportunity to study beside the sons of millionaires in an institution which once would not permit a colored man to be janitor, and in a city where the wells of Prudence Crandle were poisoned because she attempted to teach colored children. New Haven is a fine New England city. I shall always be glad of the privilege of studying New England life from the viewpoint of this city which so finely blends the ideals of education, business, and religion.

It was during this sojourn that I first saw Boston. My visit was in January, and I recall clearly the sharpness of the winds from Boston Bay as I looked out from the top of Bunker Hill Monument to the place where they had that little tea party some years ago. But I had been going to Boston for twenty years before I found the greatest place in the city. I had seen the Common, the State House, Trinity Church, the Robert Gould Shaw Monument, the Monument to Crispus Attucks, and all the rest. But one day I was rambling in the section where the streets, when duly followed out, bring you back where you started, and by accident came across this tablet on the office building at the corner of Water and Congress Streets:

135

Between Black and White

I lifted my hat and said to myself: "This is the Lake Itasca of the freedom of my people. Garrison was the father of Abolition. This is the greatest spot in America." I never go to Boston that I do not go and stand for a moment before this tablet. I took two of my daughters to Boston some time ago and showed them by the pale light of the moon the spot their father considered the greatest place in the nation. It was Garrison who began the agitation that made it possible for Lincoln to dip his pen in the blood of his heart and write the Emancipation Proclamation.

It has been a source of great gratification to me to visit the places hallowed by the footsteps of Lincoln. I spent a night in a house near the oak tree in Bloomington, Illinois, under which Mr. Lincoln made his first speech against slavery. I shall never forget the day I spent in Springfield, where Lincoln began his career. There I saw the bloodstains of the great emancipator on the white dress of Miss Keen, who took his head upon her knee soon after he was shot. In Washington I stood in the room where he died and became immortal. In Gettysburg I saw where he made his great speech for democracy, and in New Orleans I stood in the old Port Royal Hotel where he clenched his fists and swore vengeance against slavery as he saw a beautiful colored girl auctioned off.

Four times I have crossed the continent from sea to sea. Who can ever forget Niagara, appealing to eye and ear, in the world's grandest spectacle? No wonder the savages fell down before it in worship! Switzerland has nothing grander than our Rockies, the great watershed of the continent and the backbone of the nation. Every pessimist should rise in the middle of the night and climb to the top of Pike's Peak to see the sun rise, because as it beats back the darkness one gets a lesson he can never unlearn, the lesson that right is bound to overcome evil in the world. Among the wonders of the West none can be greater than the Grand Canyon, dug by the hand of the Almighty through a process of millions of years, a mile deep, thirteen miles wide and two hundred miles long! "Be still, and know that I am God."

It is an education to visit and study the cities of the United States. No two of them are alike. New York is colossal and commercial. Boston is provincial and cultured. Chicago is central and crude. Washington is political and social. Philadelphia is safe and sane. Charleston is historic and backward. Atlanta is strategic and aggressive. New Orleans is quaint and quiet. San Francisco is rugged and queer. St. Louis is rough and ready. But for sheer beauty Los Angeles excels them all. It is the Paris of America, and the garden city of the world. Coming out from the desert which borders it on the east, my wife exclaimed: "Thank God for a garden."

But of all the journeys I have made up and down, and across and back in our country, I do not recall one I enjoyed as much as I did the trip I took in a Ford for five hundred miles in the backwoods of Georgia and Alabama. With members of my family, we covered the distance in thirty days, traveling short distances each day, and stopping with friends all along the way. We scarcely had a puncture, and there was fried chicken awaiting us at every stop. The climate was delightful and the scenery as fine as anything

Traveling Through America First

I have seen in the Old World or the New. We went to the end of the railway and then nine miles beyond, just as far as a Ford could go. Then I went into the mountains to arouse my friends from whom we secured a wagon to bring in our effects. As I left the valley with the wagon I heard a pistol shot ring out, and a chicken squawked. It was her dying song. When we got back that pullet was on the table ready to eat. It was the best piece of fowl I ever tasted. The Astor House couldn't touch it!

I want here to pay my tribute to those men whose business it is to convey the public from place to place. In all my travels in the Old World and the New I cannot recall having received from any person connected with the transportation service, with possibly two exceptions, a single discourtesy. I lift my hat to the men who on trains, ships, cars, and busses carry the world in comfort and courtesy. I pay my tribute to **the Pullman porter.** I have traveled in every state in the South in **Pullman** cars, and have always received uniform courtesy and efficient service from them. In this business the colored man excels. I know of business men who defer their trip just to catch the run of certain porters. No wonder they excel: consider who many of them are — graduates, doctors,

Between Black and White

lawyers, officers, artists, ministers — driven
thither by economic necessity. A great book
will some day be written on the romance of
the Pullman porter.

SIGHTS AND SCENES IN THE
OLD WORLD

CHAPTER XII

Sights and Scenes in the Old World

THE public is proverbially ungrateful. I was surprised, therefore, when our new church was completed to receive from the people of Atlanta a thousand dollars for a trip to the Holy Land. With this sum in hand what visions came before me! From the backwoods of Tennessee to the temple at Jerusalem!

I was again surprised when I found difficulty in securing passage with touring parties on account of race prejudice, although I applied to companies in Boston as well as in New York. The problem was solved by the purchase of an independent ticket. I shall always be glad that I did this. I not only had that freedom so desirable in touring, but I had the additional pleasure of making my own bargains at hotels, thus securing cheaper rates, and also of finding my own way on reaching the various cities. This compelled me to study the history of places before reaching them and after reaching them to study the makeup of the city itself. I was in this way forced to have a clear knowledge of all I saw. It also gave me opportunity to shorten my visits in some places and to give longer time to others. It was particularly advantageous in the sacred places like Gethsemane to be alone. I was also free to rest from sight-seeing on the Sabbath, which gave me freshness in the coming week.

And yet I had plenty of company. I was with some companions for thousands of miles. Travelers abroad are not a bit snobbish and there is a great democracy among tourists. Almost everywhere I found Southern white people, and they seemed to have lost their peculiar American customs inspired by race prejudice. And by a subtle instinct I always knew them, even when we did not exchange a word. If surprise is the spice of life, my trip was indeed spicy, for it contained some very great surprises.

One of the surprises I found was the fine treatment I received on shipboard. I sailed on the good English ship *Franconia*, which was making its maiden trip down the Mediterranean. The musicians were the same ones that were playing "Nearer, My God, to Thee" when the *Titanic* went down. I had heard them play this same piece many a time on the Atlantic and the Mediterranean. After the difficulty in securing my passage I presumed I would be illtreated on shipboard. Contrary to this I was treated with the highest courtesy from the captain to the humblest steward on shipboard during the twenty-nine days I sailed on the *Franconia*. I sat at the captain's table, and a French woman sat on one side of me and a German on the other.

I wondered before leaving if I should not get lonely for people of my own color. To my surprise I saw colored people everywhere. I saw a young colored man playing on the gambling tables at Monte Carlo. One sees people of all colors in Cairo. The man who drove my carriage to the Jordan was jet black. The priest presiding at the Greek church in Tiberias was of pure ebony. I met a colored man from Virginia in Geneva. There were many colored people in Belgium. Tall black men stood at the doors of the beer gardens in Berlin. Colored people are plentiful in Paris. They seem to be at home in London. Since three-fourths of mankind belong to the colored races it ought not to be surprising to find colored people all over the world. As a matter of fact I was often taken for an American Indian, an East Indian, an Egyptian, and what not.

Although I did find colored people everywhere, I found the color line nowhere. As the skyline of New York faded out the color line faded with it. I traveled for fifteen thousand miles in the Old World and I saw nothing of racial discrimination during that time. On the other hand my color was an attraction, instead of a detraction. At Corfu, Greece, I was mistaken for a king, being the only colored man on board. It was thought that all the whites were my servants. When I found this out I refused to let the natives be told any better. Until this day they hold that a king visited their island. I was often embarrassed by being offered a suite of rooms on the presumption that I was of royal blood. No wonder a white friend of mine said that if he were colored he would save his money and make a trip abroad once every year.

My visit to Africa, which I touched first at Algiers and then at Alexandria, gave me great inspiration. I recall distinctly my first glimpse of my motherland. I arose early in the morning as our ship drew near Gibraltar, and, looking through the porthole, got my first view of Africa. There lay the head of the continent, dark, shadowy, mysterious. And it was a great day when at Algiers I put my foot for the first time on African soil. It seemed like a circus, as I rode up the Nile by rail from Alexandria to Cairo, to see plows drawn by dromedaries, zebras and other animals. What a scene is presented in the streets of Cairo, a veritable midway of all nations! What contrasts are presented in this ancient city of Egypt! Here is a cart drawn by a camel, while a modern automobile whisks by. There is a woman dressed as in the time of the Pharaohs, while by her side is a woman dressed as stylishly as any woman in Paris. Behold a face jet black, and another as white as snow! Houses ancient and modern stand side by side. Cairo is a veritable city of contrasts, and her streets are aflame with color.

One morning at Yale Dean Day said that the only time the colored race was mentioned in the Bible was that in which reference is made to the inability of the leopard to change his spots or the Ethiopian his skin. My Baedeker, however, referred to a certain bust in the Egyptian museum as having the features of a Negro. The next morning when I visited the Cairo museum I looked for this bust of Tarhaka, one of the Bible kings, and saw that he had the full features of a Negro. I looked up on the wall, and saw the pictures of white, brown, and black kings and queens, the builders of ancient Egypt. At Gizeh, the Sphinx, with a smile that would not come off though swept by the sands of seventy centuries, bore the likeness of a Negro. At Memphis I saw the full length basalt statue of Rameses the Second, the grandson of that Pharaoh before whom Moses pleaded to let his people go. It was the statue of a big black man. Since my visit further explorations confirm the fact that black men and women took a leading part in the making of ancient Egypt, the mother of modern civilization. Coming up from Africa, I got a new pride in my race that I have never forgotten. My race did not come from the jungles; it came through the jungles. It came from palaces and thrones, and kings and queens.

It is only a night's ride from Africa to the Holy Land. Touching this sacred land at Joppa, where the scenes of Jonah were laid, an afternoon's journey by rail through the midst of historic scenes in the hills of Judea brings one to the walls of Jerusalem. For once I wanted to be a porter, as he exclaimed: "Jerusalem!" There I was in the Holy City, six thousand miles from home. A ten-minute's carriage ride takes us from the station on the outskirts of the city through the gates into the city where David ruled and Jesus was crucified. My hotel was right opposite the palace where David sat on his throne. Going to the top of the hotel of the New Jerusalem I saw the city at my feet just as the prophet had spoken of it: "As the hills are round about Jerusalem, so is the Lord round about his people." I was happy to

148

live on that side of the hotel where morning, noon, and night I could look out on Gethsemane and Calvary. In the evening a man walks out and hangs a lantern in the shape of a cross in the tower of the Church of the Holy Sepulcher. It is the only light that illumines the city at night. I thought of Bowring's hymn: "In the cross of Christ I glory."

What days these were! The day at Bethlehem, where I laid my hand on the star that marks the spot where the Babe was born. The day down at the Jordan, where Christ was baptized. The day at Bethany, where he raised Lazarus from the dead. The day in Gethsemane, where we sit alone as we recreate the scene. The day at Calvary, where the vision of the crucified One reappears. The day on the way to Emmaus, when we try to put our feet in the steps our Lord must have made. The day in the temple, when we put our hands on the rock where Abraham started to offer up Isaac. Jerusalem, the very ground seems holy!

After a week's sojourn we turn our faces northward, and for three days we travel horseback through the Holy Land. Passing the point where Mary discovered the loss of the little Christ, we come in the afternoon to Jacob's well, and at night we go to our tent midway between Gerizim and Ebal, symbols of the blessing and the curse. That evening at sunset we climbed Gerizim to see the ancient sect of the Samaritans sacrifice as in the olden day, believing that the Messiah is yet to come. Another day through the mountains of Samaria brings us to Jenin, where we spend the night in a tent, while jackals bark all around us. The next day we travel through the valley of the Jezreel, all billowy with the grain growing in the soil made red by the blood of many a battle between Israel and her foes. The night brings us to the Greek monastery on the top of Mt. Tabor, where many think the Son of God was transfigured. From this height we may see the little city of Nain, the Fountain of Gideon, Mt. Carmel, and the city of Nazareth, where Christ was brought up. It is Easter, and the night finds us in the city of Joseph and Mary, and on the morrow we seek the little carpenter shops like those in which Jesus must have worked. From Nazareth we go to the city of Cana, where the Master wrought his first miracle; and from thence, twenty miles away, we come to the Sea of Galilee. Escaping the hands of robbers on the outskirts of the city, where Jesus gave the great sermon of his life, we come to Tiberias, where we dine with a Turkish governor. The next day we sail on the sea the Master loved. There it is like a mirror in a big brown frame, six miles long and thirteen miles wide. Our approach the afternoon before had furnished a scene one could never forget. The rain had passed, and a reflection came up from the deep basin that filled the sky with tints of wondrous beauty. Above was the pure white of the ever-living snows of Mt. Hermon, while beyond was the deep blue of the mountains of Moab. Over all spanned the rainbow with its variegated colors, making a scene that will remain in the memory as long as one lives. Sailing for a day on the sea where Jesus taught and quelled the storm, it was hard to imagine the place without seeing the Master walking on the turbulent waves, saying: "Peace, be still." There were the ruins of the cities he upbraided, Capernaum, Chorazin, Bethsaida. In the twilight of the early morning I saw the sea as the mists hung over it, reminding one of the time when Jesus walked on the shore, pulled down fire from the stars, and cooked the breakfast for the cold, hungry, wet disciples who had toiled all night and caught nothing. I saw him as he served the food he had prepared for them.

A day's ride takes us through Bozrah to Damascus, the oldest city in the world, and a real garden city. It is spoon-shaped, and our station is at the end of the handle while our hotel is at the end of the bowl. A ride through the rough, stony streets brings us to the hotel just under Mt. Kasyoun, which we climb next day. From there we see toward the purple east the stair steps of the Libyan Mountains. To the west we see Mt. Hermon clad in ever-living snow. Nine miles away is the village of Kokeb, where Paul saw his vision. At our feet lies the city, through which runs the Urbana River, split into seven different branches and again uniting into one at the lower end of the city. Filled with flowers, pomegranates and nuts, Damascus is the garden city of the world. The following day finds us in the Street that is called Straight, ending at the house where Paul was baptized. Who can forget the bazaars of Damascus, where the Mohammedan merchants pray and cheat you at the same time!

From Damascus I came by way of Baalbec across the mountains of Lebanon to Beirut, Syria, where I was the guest of President Bliss of the American Syrian Protestant College. I shall never forget the audience of black-eyed, snappy students, about 1,000 in number, to whom I had the privilege of speaking. I told them of the beginning of schools in the South at about the same time their college was opened. But at the request of the teachers I refrained from telling them anything of the seamy side of the interracial life in the United States. I was greatly delighted with the cordial reception I received from the students in my address in the afternoon and in another address at night in the Y. M. C. A., when the students packed the doors and windows to see and hear the dark-skinned man from America. The touch of color made us kin.

Time will fail me to tell of Athens, where I stood with Paul on Mars Hill; of Constantinople, the city of three Sundays, where I saw the sultan go to church; of Florence, where I sat in the tower where Savonarola spent his last hours before execution; of Venice, where I heard a sermon with water as its theme; of Milan, the last city in Italy before we enter the Simplon tunnel penetrating the Alps; of Geneva, the seat of the League of Nations today; of Paris, the most beautiful city in the world; of Rome, seated on her seven hills; of Berlin, the home of the former kaiser; of Brussels, the storm center of the World War; of London, where I witnessed the coronation of King George.

But the finest thing I saw abroad was at Liverpool. It was the ship that brought me home. That greyhound of the sea, the *Mauretania*, could not travel too fast for me, and I was glad at the end of five days to land in the harbor of New York. There the sun seemed to shine brighter, the air to blow freer, and the people to look happier than in any place I had been since I left these shores. When I saw our flag floating to the breeze I knew in the depths of my heart that I was an American through and through. With all her faults I still loved my country. I had a truer feeling of what John Howard Payne meant when he sang: "There is no place like home."

ON THE TRAIL OF THE COLORED
DOUGHBOY

CHAPTER XIII

On the Trail of the Colored Doughboy

I HAVE never been able to see soldiers going off to war without wishing to go with them. This feeling came to its highest intensity when I saw so many colored men going to the World War. Atlanta was the center for the gathering of the Southeastern quota, and the city was so alive with the war spirit that it permeated everything. For one thing it packed our churches with people interested in the great spectacle across the sea. Over fifty boys went from my church alone.

I was moved to offer my services as chaplain in case of need, but the age limit barred me, and I gave up all hope to taking part in the great war. Imagine my surprise after the armistice was signed to receive a telegram from the headquarters of General Pershing requesting me to come to France to help sustain the morale of the boys left behind to clean up the debris of the war. The matter was laid before my church and they generously permitted me to go.

After the adjustment of preliminaries with

157

Between Black and White

the Young Men's Christian Association I sailed on the *George Washington* early in March, 1919, landing at Brest, France. From there I went to Paris, where I made my head-quarters for three months. I traveled four thousand miles in the French Republic, visit-ing all the battlefields and speaking to one hundred thousand colored soldiers.

My unit, which was the only one of its kind, consisted of Professor J. E. Blanton, of South Carolina, as singer, and Miss Helen Hagan, of New Haven, Connecticut, as pian-ist. Professor Blanton would lead the men in singing, and in turn would sing to them. The transformation of these dejected men was almost instantaneous when they forgot themselves in song. The change was still greater when Miss Hagan would appear and play upon the piano. In many cases, they had not seen a woman of their own race since they left home, and frequently tears would swell up in the eyes of these men as they looked upon this talented woman.

After the soil was prepared by music I attempted to sow the seed. I have never spoken to such large audiences. They would fill the auditoriums to suffocation, jam the windows and doors, climb up onto the roofs and fill the skylights. In one case at Brest, where we held a meeting in the main auditorium, it was necessary to have two meetings. Three thousand came in for the first service, and when they marched out three thousand more came. Each service continued an hour and a half.

I have never found audiences more enthusiastic and responsive. It was my custom to speak to the men humorously for half an hour, and then to take up the more serious things of life. I would call to the platform five young men to help me deliver the message. Each one of these would stand for a point I wanted to make. The first would stand for "Train your brain"; second, "Save your money"; third, "Make friends"; fourth, "Get a wife"; fifth, "Join the church." These were the things they were to do on their return home. I have rarely spoken since that time in any part of America that I have not had some young veteran come up to me and tell me that he heard me in France; and in many cases, told me of the points he had followed out. In one case, for instance, I carried a letter from a young lady in Atlanta to a soldier in Is-sur-Tille, and on his return home I had the pleasure of performing their ceremony in marriage and of receiving him into the fellowship of the church of which she was already a member.

Speaking in round numbers, a million

Between Black and White

colored men were called in the selective draft of the World War, a half million put on the uniform, and a quarter of a million went overseas. Our unit had the privilege of ministering to one hundred thousand of these, sometimes by the wayside, sometimes standing deep in mud, sometimes in the rain, sometimes in barracks. Under all circumstances, they were cheerful and optimistic but longing to return home.

The colored soldiers made a very fine impression on the French people. In all my journeyings over the battlefields and through the near-by cities I never heard a single complaint by any Frenchman of the *soldat noir*. It was a remarkable thing that a colored person could approach a Frenchman anywhere without an introduction, and almost immediately be on terms of *bon homme*. I believe the Negro and the French are affinities. They are both emotional, artistic, musical, fun-loving, and religious. Perhaps that is why they understand each other so quickly. Then, too, it seemed to me that the French appreciated the fact that the American Negro had come overseas to fight for that democracy for others which he had never had for himself. This was accentuated by the fact that some Americans drew a line on color even in France, — that always inexplicable

160

thing to the French mind. The French not only believe in liberty, equality, and fraternity for themselves but also for other people, and they were quick to resent any injustice by the white Americans against colored Americans.

The colored soldiers soon caught the spirit of the French people, and resented any discrimination on racial grounds. I saw a riot in Romaigne because of this very thing. The Young Men's Christian Association had drawn the color line in the service of the soldiers at their canteen. The Knights of Columbus sympathized with the colored boys and asked them to come to them with the assurance that no color line would be drawn in their service. The colored boys responded, but in a few days the Knights also put up signs drawing the color line. This so angered the colored boys that they tore the tent down. The situation became very tense until the colored guards were called, and their presence soon brought peace out of confusion. But the incident broke up the color line signs in Romaigne.

Colored soldiers made an excellent record for their race in France. They broke the record as laborers, doing within six months what the French working man declared would require six years to do. It was the arm of the black man that aided in the quick transportation of food, clothing, arms, and other supplies from the coast to the trenches, thus bringing the war to an earlier termination. They made a record as fighters, colored men being the first to receive that highest decoration for bravery. They made a record as officers. A thousand colored men wore shoulder straps, and they brought back wonderful records for bravery.

A colored private came back from the front at Metz fatally wounded. As the blood gushed from his wounds, the colored surgeon asked him how he got them. "I got them," he said, "following a colored officer who had not gone very far in his studies." "What do you mean?" inquired the surgeon. "My lieutenant did not go far enough in his studies to learn the word retreat. He fell on my broken arm and he lies up there now with his eyes on Metz. Doctor, get me well so that I may go back and carry on where my lieutenant fell!" Before I left Atlanta the father of this officer came to me and said: "Doctor, don't come back until you have found the grave of my boy." At last I found it in Thiacourt near the flagpole from which the Stars and Stripes float proudly. I picked up a little stone and brought it all the way back to give to that father, whose son had not

HENRY HUGH PROCTOR
As he was known to the Colored Soldiers in France

gone far enough in his studies to learn the word retreat.

Six children were born to us in the parsonage in Atlanta hard by the church — Henry, Richard, Muriel, Lillian, Roy, and Vashti, mentioned in the order of their birth. The selective draft commandeered the first-born just as he had completed his college course at Fisk. After a period of training at Des Moines, he was made a first lieutenant and in due season sailed for France. After many narrow escapes, he faced death on the last day of the battle. Sent to clean out a machine gun nest, he was cut off from the main part of his regiment and only a screen of smoke preserved him from the enemy. He could neither go forward nor backward, and he felt that he had to stand and die as the creeping barrage of fire drew near. Observing his watch, he thought he had only fifteen minutes to live. At the end of that time he heard the German bugle blow on one side, and on the other the band playing the Star Spangled Banner — and the war was over! He ascribed his deliverance to prayer. He was right. Without his knowledge his mother was joined by a white woman a thousand miles away to pray daily for the safe return of that boy. And he came back home without a scratch, thanks to prayer between Black and White.

Between Black and White

The most sacred task of the war was committed to the hands of the colored doughboy. In the haste of battle the dead were often buried by the roadside, some with their faces downward, and others were left unburied in the forests. These colored boys picked up those by the roadside, scurried the forests for the unburied, and took up those improperly interred. They assembled the bodies in the cemeteries which are the most beautiful spots in La Belle, France. Over each grave stands a white cross with the name and company of the soldier engraved on it. What a wonderful sight to see those boys march up the hillsides bearing the crosses to the resting-places of the sacred dead! It reminds us of that other sacred scene in history when an African bore the cross of Christ up the little green hill far away.

It was a privilege for me to shake the hands of these boys laden with the aroma of the dead. I said to them: "Boys, I am proud of you. You have done the most sacred task of the war. What others have refused to do, you have done willingly and beautifully. I promise you that when I go back home I will speak to no audience that I do not tell them of what you have done." And then I added: "America will not forget!"

THE HIDDEN MEANING OF THE NEGRO MIGRATION

CHAPTER XIV

The Hidden Meaning of the Negro Migration

THE trend of the world is toward larger liberty, and the upshot of the World War was the making of this ideal the heritage of every man, woman, and child on the globe. The first shot in that transatlantic tragedy was heard around the world, and the appeal for the victory of democracy awoke the sleeping peon in the backwoods of the South.

But as the hands of the clock swing from one extreme to the other, this tide of the high-water mark of world liberty had its reaction. Even in the midst of the war murmurings of the reactionaries could be heard in the South. Men began to fear what the Negro, long kept back from his rightful liberty and having drunk the draughts of freedom beyond the seas, would expect. In anticipation of this there were deep-laid plans to curb his spirit.

As a fruit of these machinations we had riots in such cities as Chicago, Omaha, East St. Louis, and even Washington itself. But in these cities Negroes who had fought in the war overseas showed themselves equally brave here, and they pledged themselves, having assisted in the conquest of the Hun across the ocean, to stop the Hun at home. It is hardly likely that similar riots will take place in our day. A burnt child is afraid of the fire.

The mob routed in the open took to cover, and we have the revival of the Ku Klux Klan, that un-American, undemocratic brigade of the pillow-case. I was born within twelve miles of the place where the original Klan started. Its original purpose was to frighten the Negro by appealing to what was supposed to be his sense of fear of the invisible. But the psychology of that is now out-of-date, and the man who went through the horrors of the Argonne is not likely to be frightened by a coward with a nightgown. To strengthen their scheme the Ku Klux have included Jews, Catholics, and other elements that may have incurred local disfavor. But they have taken in too much territory, and their plan, based on private vengeance and force, will fail because it cannot stand the light of pure Americanism. Men love darkness rather than light because their deeds are evil, and evil is temporary. Expose it, and it will die.

This reactionary movement, however, has had two distinct results. The first was to inspire the Negro to greater efforts at self-betterment in the South. The Negro has made more progress in the South in the short period since the World War than he did in ten times the same period before the war. His strides in business, home building, and cooperative endeavor have been almost phenomenal.

But this was not the only result. All Negroes are not alike, and different types react differently, as is the case with other people. So there was another result of this reactionary movement: the redistribution of the Negro population in America. Since the last census the geographical center of Negro population has moved from a point near Atlanta northward to a point near Chattanooga, one hundred and fifty miles away.

Even if a race that has under untoward circumstances accumulated a billion dollars since its manumission a little over a half century ago could be called shiftless, it certainly could not be called shifting in view of the fact that practically ninety per cent of them remained for nearly three centuries in that section where their ancestors first entered America. The fact, then, that there has been a large movement of these people to another section within the last few years indicates that there are some deep-seated causes for such action. Among these causes, I name three 'n passing.

Between Black and White

The first is the ill-treatment accorded the colored people in the South. This does not mean that there are not many good white people in the South. As a matter of fact, they are in the majority. But it does mean that the good did not sufficiently assert themselves to restrain the bad in their treatment of the blacks. As a result certain types of Negroes got tired of being treated in the southern way, and moved, not in anger for the most part, but because they were grieved. With all its faults the Negro loves the South, though he hates many of its customs. It is his ancestral home. His forbears felled its forests, planted its fields, spanned its streams with bridges, worked in its mines, tenderly nursed its children, and the bodies of their sacred dead lie buried in its soil.

But this is not all. Coupled with it was the call of the North. That section had relied largely on foreign labor, but when the World War broke out many of these returned to their native colors. This, together with the increased demand for the manufacture of explosives and other war material, made an unusual demand for labor at very high prices. With pressure in the rear and a glittering invitation in the front, it is not surprising that the Negro should get up and leave, a million or more strong. There was a stirring in the

170

Hidden Meaning of the Negro Migration

South almost like that in Egypt in the days
of old.

But there is still another reáson not often
sensed by one not of Negro blood, — a desire
on the part of this long-suppressed people for
self-realization in the American democracy.
This was the most favorable opportunity
offered them in history for equality of opportunity, and their newly found American
instinct bade them seize it. The opportunity
for the education of their children, for the
casting of the ballot untrammeled, for freedom from restriction in travel and public
places and the harassing of mobs, made a
tremendous appeal to these Americans who
had never lifted their hands against the Stars
and the Stripes.

Nor has the movement yet ceased. It is
not as spectacular as it was, but is still going
on. Relatives are constantly sending back
for those left behind, and in most cases they
have jobs for them before they leave home.
As a result there is a constant redistribution
of the American Negro going on. There is
scarcely a corner of the land where one cannot today find colored immigrants from the
South. I found some recently as far up in
the Northwest as Bellingham, Washington,
and they were doing well.

Progress does not mean the decrease but

the increase of problems. This new distri-
bution of a people brings a distinctly new
problem into American life. No longer is the
problem of the white and colored races a local
problem. It is a national problem. The
Negro, used to the provincial life of the
South, must adjust himself to the larger life
of the nation. This is no small problem when
it is considered that his life has hitherto been
with a people of homogeneous stock. Now
he must come into touch with people from
every race under heaven. He must also face
a new and rigid climate, which is no small test
for these children of the South with its won-
derfully mild climate. Then, too, they must
be measured by different laws and customs,
which is a great ordeal to a simple, warm-
hearted race. And yet this very thing means
the larger education and affords the needed
discipline for an easy-going group.

It is not always understood that an ad-
vanced civilization holds new perils for an
undeveloped people. The Africans on the
coast are in greater peril than their brethren
in the interior, since the primitive life has its
own conservative forces which are lacking in
a semi-civilized type of life. And the Negroes
in our South are in greater peril than the
African on the coast, because the South
offers a still higher civilization than the bor-

der of heathenism. By the same token the Negro in the North is in even greater peril than his brethren in the South. He is in danger of getting the corrupting instead of the saving influences of this higher civilization.

In this situation there is but one thing that will save him, and that is his church. With the Saxon the home antedated the church, but with the African it is just the reverse. The church, therefore, has a place in the life of the Negro that is primary. The Negro has a genius for religion, and the church is the guaranty of the preservation of the religious life of the race.

In a recent journey across the continent I was struck with three things in regard to the church life of my people. The first was that though they had free entrance into the white churches they preferred, as a rule, churches of their own where they could develop their own worship. Another thing was that their churches as social centers of the group were crowded morning and night. And the other was the inadequacy of the present type of religious life for the proper development of the race. The present type of religion offered to the colored people is individualistic and sentimental; whereas what is needed is a new type of religious life which

173

centers about teaching, preaching, healing; teaching, the ministry to the mind; preaching, the ministry to the soul; healing, the ministry to the body. That is the type of religion my people need today!

I have made this long detour to explain why, after twenty-five years in the heart of the South, where I built up a church that was very dear to me and fell in love with a city that was very good to me, I reluctantly broke the sacred ties of a lifetime to follow the Northward trail of my people. I caught a vision of a chain of churches stretching from the Statue of Liberty to the Golden Gate that would function in the entire life of the colored people. I am endeavoring to forge the first link of this chain right under the shadow of the Statue of Liberty, and it is a joy to note the beginnings of others scattered from coast to coast. Recently I covered the entire distance from sea to sea, speaking to each one of these little groups, at Buffalo, Painesville, Cleveland, Detroit, Chicago, Des Moines, St. Louis, Los Angeles. Trans-continental bonfires to illuminate the paths of a people in the perils of the North!

THE DAWN OF A NEW DAY

CHAPTER XV

The Dawn of a New Day

CLEAR thinking on the problem of the races becomes greatly simplified when it is recognized that the problem has two sides, the White and the Black side. Effective action claims a similar clarification when it is realized that neither side can successfully assume the responsibilities of the other. Of course, there is a realm where both must work together in view of the resultant due to their relationship, but it is clear that operation must precede cooperation. While they must bear one another's burdens, each must bear its own and work out its own salvation.

Failure to recognize these fundamental truths has resulted in some glaring errors in our efforts at solving our problem. One of these has been too much dependence on the White. No race has ever solved the problem of another. Another mistake has been too much dependence on the efficacy of the law. Beneath all law lies public sentiment, without which a mere statute is valueless. Still another error has been reliance upon our leaders to work out our problems for us.

Between Black and White

But leaders never solved the problems of
people; they can only point the way. It is
for the people to work out their own salvation.

This is the conclusion of the whole matter:
The colored people must work out their own
problem, under the guidance of their own
leaders, and in cooperation with the better
elements of the white American. I have a
profound faith in the native wisdom of my
people. They have a rare philosophy all
their own. I am increasingly impressed with
the unselfish devotion of the true leaders of
the colored race. Their self-abnegation has
rarely been equalled in history. I have an
abiding faith in the better of the white men
of America, despite the fact that there still
occur many things contrary to the genius of
our institutions.

I believe in the right kind of agitation. Of
course, there is a false kind, the kind that is
negative, producing within the colored people
an unnatural pessimism and irritating the
white to no purpose. On the other hand,
there is a constructive agitation without
which there can be no progress. I do not
think that lectures read to colored people by
white people do very much good; nor do I
think lectures read by colored to white people
do very much good. If we could have a
gentleman's agreement to let the colored do

178

the lecturing to their own people and the white to theirs, I feel confident we would get along much faster than by the present all too prevalent method. If each race will take the beam out of its own eye, then it could see more clearly to take the mote out of its brother's eye.

A certain white poet has called the black man the white man's burden, and in turn a certain black poet has called the white man the black man's burden. Both are wrong. It is true the white man has not always been as tender in dealing with his colored brother as he should but, on the whole, it must be admitted in all fairness that the white man has been a blessing and not a curse to his brother in black. And while the colored man has not always measured up to the ideal expected of him, candor compels us to say that his association with the white man in America has been a blessing and not a curse.

Historically, there have been three attempts in the South to solve the problem of the races. The first was just after the Civil War when the black man tried it by himself, and although during this much abused period the erring states were received back into the Union, the ballot box opened to all on the basis of manhood, and the public school door swung open to all for the first time, yet it failed of its highest fruition because it lacked the cooperation of the white man. A quarter of a century later another effort was made to solve the problem, when the white man tried it by himself; and although during this period there was a new stirring of patriotism in the South, a renaissance of industrialism and a new impetus to education, yet this period fell short of its promise because it lacked the cooperation of the black man. In Grady's dream of the New South there was no adequate place for the progressive Negro. Any attempt to solve the problem of the races in the South without the cooperation of both races is doomed to failure. Now, at length, there is another attempt, not by the white man alone, nor by the black alone, but by both.

This third way rests on the universal principle for the solution of all social problems and is bound to succeed. Its application should not be confined to the South. It is the only way it can be solved in any part of our land. The South has discovered through much tribulation the principle for the solution of this problem not only in our own land, but for all the world, and it is significant that those seeking solution for similar problems in other parts of the world are studying America's plan of interracial cooperation. This

The Dawn of a New Day

puts upon us a new responsibility and opportunity.

We have the opportunity of working out on American soil the new ideal of brotherhood in black and white. The black man and the white are contrasts, not contraries; complementary opposites, not irreconcilable opponents. Their interests are identical, their destinies inseparable. The one eternal lesson for them both to learn is how better they can love one another. In all cooperative effort love is basic.

When I was about to leave the South, my people came about me and said, "Are you deserting us?" My reply was, "No, never." Unless I had felt that I could have done more for my people in the North than in the South I should never have left the South. New York is the United States in miniature. It is the center of the commercial, political, educational, social and religious life of the nation. New York is the place to center any movement that affects the nation and the world. Just now there is getting under way in the metropolis a new organization known as "The National Conference on the Christian Way of Life," which proposes to restate the Christian conception in its application to the social problems of the day.

Prominent among these problems is that of

the relationship between the races. This organization is composed of one hundred or more men and women from all parts of the country, and the thorough methods of its procedure, the wide scope of its inquiry, and the noble motives at its base seem to guarantee its ultimate success. I regard my membership in this organization as one of the best opportunities that has come to me to help my brethren in the dark and remote corners of the South, the nation, and the world.

Evidently, we are on the borderland of a new world, not only in the application of modern science to the progress of mankind from a physical viewpoint, but also in the application of the things of the spirit to the social relationships of men. Old things are passing away; all things are being made new. Old delusions are being discarded. Men no longer believe that hate will solve our problems. The idea of brute force is losing ground and war is doomed. The idea that one race may be down, that another may be up, is exploded. The theory of all men up is found to be sound. In the true light of life we are seeing things in a new relationship. The sun is rising, and we are in the dawn of a new day.

THE OUTLOOK

CHAPTER XVI
The Outlook

IT is a mistake to assume that all the white slave-holders were of the type of Legree. My mother often told me how kind and gentle her owners were. Mrs. Stowe does not fail to pay her tribute to this class. But notwithstanding the existence of many slavers who were kind and good within their limitations, the South, despite heroes like John G. Fee of Kentucky, who freed their slaves, was unable to solve the problem of slavery. It had to be solved by the North and then applied to the South. Now the enlightened portion of the South would not exchange the new era of freedom for the old régime of slavery. But the North had first to make an ocular demonstration of the superiority of freedom over slavery and then enforce its ideal.

It is also a mistake to assume that all the white people of the South today are of the type of the late Benjamin Tillman. There is a new school of whites in the South like the late John J. Eagan of Atlanta, one of the noblest Americans of this generation. They are trying to do the right thing by their colored fellow citizens. Their conduct is frequently heroic. But notwithstanding this fact, the South as a whole is as unable to solve the problem that confronts it today as it was the problem that confronted it over a half century ago. This is a national problem and it cannot be solved on sectional lines. It must be solved in the broad light of American principle. Sectional temporizing will fail. Hampered by tradition, handicapped by ignorance, enthralled by poverty, the South is unable to solve this problem in the only way it can be solved. History is, therefore, repeating itself; and it is again up to the North to give the nation an example of the solution.

Providential indications point this way. On account of the post-war depression, Congress reduced foreign immigration to a minimum. With the return of prosperity there was a shortage of labor in our industries. At the same time the boll-weevil, beginning his ravages in Texas, crossed the Mississippi, traversed Alabama, and is now marching through Georgia. With one hand over the sea, holding the foreigner back, and the other over the South, beckoning the black man hither, Providence seems to be making its meaning unusually clear.

In the redistribution of the American Negro, he is moving Northward in three parallel columns. From the Southwest there is one column sweeping along the Pacific Coast, the head of which is centering around Los Angeles and San Francisco. From the Central South it is sweeping up the Mississippi Valley, centering around Chicago and Detroit. From the Southeast it is sweeping up the Atlantic Seaboard, centering about Philadelphia and New York.

I was deeply stirred when I stood some years ago at Ellis Island, and saw immigrants from the Old World coming up out of the steerage. As they saluted the flag upon entering this land of opportunity the light of new hope played upon their faces. But one day in the Union Station at Washington I was stirred still more deeply as I saw two hundred colored people who had just arrived from the South. Presently they departed, some going to Philadelphia, others to New York, and others to Boston. Within a few minutes a similar group came on another train. They consisted of young men with their wives and children, and on their faces there played a light that never was on land or sea. Plainly, they were seeking a better country.

In the end I believe this movement will be beneficial to all concerned. It will help the North by providing that section with home-made workers. It will be found that right at our doors is all the help we need. It will help the South by ridding it of surplus labor and by giving it an opportunity to substitute machinery for drudgery. This will lift the general average of intelligence of black and white. It will help the Southern Negro by giving him the outlet for the larger life he has been seeking. It will help the Northern Negro by giving him a larger natural constituency for business and social development. It will help the nation by standardizing the race problem. Every time a Negro crosses the Mason and Dixon Line from the South he broadens the base of the American democracy.

But, as I have said, the chief opportunity of the North is to give the South a practical demonstration of the gospel of equal opportunity it has so nobly and sincerely preached. This I believe the North is minded to do. Her chief temptation is the lure of the Ku Klux spirit. I believe she will resist it, and preserve her true American spirit. She is the custodian of the American ideal, and her infidelity is unthinkable.

If the North makes this demonstration, as I believe she will, eventually the South will turn her passion into compassion, and go the North one better. The Southerner is not so quick to see a situation, but once he sees it and it appeals to him, he will take hold of it with a passion unknown to the Northerner. He is all one way or the other. The sporadic attempts he is now making to solve the race problem along the higher lines will become general, and the South will become the garden spot of the nation and the paradise of the races. It requires no prophet to stand on her hills and see the coming kingdom of interracial cooperation. The hills once red with the blood of strife will glow with a new light.

Once the South takes up the example of the North, this section will rid itself of the curse of the Klan spirit, and we shall present to the world an example for the solution of its greatest problem, the question of color. Three-fourths of mankind are colored, and there can be no world peace until this question is settled in the only way, that of the Golden Rule of Christ.

Thus I see the rainbow of hope like a silken scarf spanning the shoulder of the dying storm of racial hate, blending into one every color under the sun — one race, the human; one language, the English; one religion, the Christian.